W9-BAR-037

200 budget meals

200 budget meals

hamlyn **all color**

Sunil Vijayakar

An Hachette UK Company
www.hachette.co.uk

First published in Great Britain in 2008 by Hamlyn,
a division of Octopus Publishing Group Ltd
Endeavour House, 189 Shaftesbury Avenue,
London WC2H 8JY
www.octopusbooksusa.com

Distributed in the U.S. and Canada by Octopus Books USA:
c/o Hachette Book Group
237 Park Avenue
New York NY 10017

Some of the recipes in this book have previously
appeared in the following books published by Hamlyn:
Fab Fast Food by Sunil Vijayakar and *30-minute Vegetarian*
by Joanna Farrow

ISBN: 978-0-600-61949-9

A CIP catalog record for this book is available
from the Library of Congress

Printed and bound in China

3 4 5 6 7 8 9 10

Standard level spoon measurements are used in all recipes.

Ovens should be preheated to the specified temperature.
If using a fan-assisted oven, follow the manufacturer's
instructions for adjusting the time and temperature.

Eggs should be medium unless otherwise stated. The Food
and Drug Administration advises that eggs should not be
consumed raw. This book contains some dishes made with
raw or lightly cooked eggs. It is prudent for more vulnerable
people, such as pregnant and nursing mothers, invalids,
the elderly, babies, and young children, to avoid uncooked
or lightly cooked dishes made with eggs.

This book includes dishes made with nuts and nut derivatives.
It is advisable for those with known allergic reactions to nuts
and nut derivatives and those who may be potentially
vulnerable to these allergies, such as pregnant and nursing
mothers, invalids, the elderly, babies, and children, to avoid
dishes made with nuts and nut oils. It is also prudent to
check the labels of pre-prepared ingredients for the possible
inclusion of nut derivatives.

contents

introduction

introduction

Just because you're watching your wallet, that doesn't mean you have to miss out on fabulous food. This sensational collection of recipes has been specially created for busy people who want no-fuss meals made from great ingredients that won't break the bank. There's everything from simple appetizers and snacks to healthy salads and vegetable dishes, hearty main meals, and sumptuous desserts. So, whatever you're in the mood for, even if you're on a budget, there's something here to satisfy and enjoy.

Fabulous food on a budget
The secret of creating really delicious meals every time lies in the choice of ingredients.

If you choose good-quality ingredients, it's very hard to go wrong. And the key point is that quality doesn't have to mean additional expense. If you know where to look and what to look for, it's easy to buy fantastic-tasting ingredients economically. So what's the secret?

Spend more to spend less
Sometimes it's worth spending a little extra on a more expensive ingredient because in the long run you'll end up using less of it. For example, Italian Parmesan cheese or a really well-flavored cheddar cheese might be more expensive than a block of cheap American cheese, but the flavor is so rich and intense that you only need to use a small amount. If you are making a cheese sauce, for instance, you would need to use far less of the more expensive cheese to achieve a full-flavored sauce than you would a mild, tasteless one, so weight for weight and price for price, the Parmesan or cheddar will work out to be a much better buy.

Choose wisely: meat and poultry
These ingredients can really bump up the cost of your meal, but clever shopping can mean luxurious meals that don't cost the earth. When it comes to inexpensive—and quick—eats, ground meat is always a great choice because it's incredibly versatile as well

as very economical and speedy, being perfect for meatballs, kebabs, sauces, curries, and bakes, to name but a few options. But there are other cheaps cuts that are good too. Pork is generally a reasonably priced meat and pork leg steaks make a great, lean choice, but even more expensive cuts such as prime tenderloin steak can be made economical by your choice of dish. For example, take a small piece of expensive beef tenderloin, slice it very thinly, and then stir-fry it with plenty of vegetables and you'll have a memorable meal with delicious meat but for very little cost.

Both poultry and meat can be "stretched" by bulking them out with other cheaper ingredients such as beans, rice, pasta, and noodles, as in Rice Noodles with Lemon Chicken, page 144, and Quick Sausage & Bean Casserole, page 146. And you can cut costs with poultry by buying a whole bird

and jointing it yourself, rather than buying individual portions. Alternatively, you can buy cheaper portions such as thighs and drumsticks in bulk and freeze what you don't need for a later date—they can be cooked in delicious dishes such as Fast Chicken Curry, page 132, and Tandoori Chicken, page 156.

Choose wisely: fish and shellfish
Like meat and poultry, fish and shellfish can be pricey, so be prepared to buy what looks good and is well priced on your fish merchant's slab or on the supermarket counter on the day. Fish and shellfish should usually be eaten on the day you purchase them and must be in excellent condition, so check for fresh-smelling fish with shiny skins, bright eyes, and firm flesh. As a general rule, avoid buying fish on a Monday. Fish that often offer especially good value for money include salmon, trout, sardines, and mackerel. Although some shellfish and seafood such as fresh crab and lobster are expensive, others—notably mussels and squid—are relatively cheap as well as quick to cook, versatile, and delicious.

Buy in season
Fresh fruit and vegetables are at their absolute best when they're in season. Ripe, succulent, sweet, and juicy—not only do they taste great but they're available in abundance, so are usually better priced. Out of season

ingredients often have an inferior taste and are invariably more expensive because they are scarce. Also, they have frequently been flown in from far-flung places, which again pushes up the price. It's usually true to say that the less-traveled and fresher an ingredient is, the better it will be, so buying locally grown produce is often a good way of ensuring that it's fresh, which in turn reduces the risk of wastage.

But, whether you're buying in-season or imported produce, make sure that your items of choice look in good condition before purchasing. If fruit and vegetables appear tired and wilted, it's a good rule of thumb to assume that they're past their best, so always choose the freshest-, firmest-looking specimens. If the leaves are attached, they should be green and fresh looking. Don't

worry whether the produce is perfectly round and uniform, but do make sure that it's not bruised, soft, or wrinkled.

Opt for fruit and/or vegetable boxes
One of the easiest ways to get healthy, seasonal, good-quality fruit and/or vegetables —and without even having to spend money on transport—is with a box delivery scheme. Check out a local scheme in your area to have locally grown, seasonal fruit and vegetables delivered direct to your door. They offer a wide selection of produce and, because everything's in season and grown locally, it should prove good value for money.

Select own-brand products
Although cost can often indicate quality, this isn't always the case, and cheaper own-brand products are often just as good as the more expensive branded ones. Shop around and decide for yourself what's worth spending more on and when the cheaper option is just as good.

Stocking up your pantry
A well-stocked pantry is essential for any cook, but when you're looking to put together meals on a budget it's even more important. You don't want to find yourself ready to start cooking only to realize that you're missing an all-important ingredient and have to pop out to the nearest and maybe more expensive shop, thereby costing you extra money and

time. And if you keep a good pantry you can take advantage of all kinds of offers in the supermarket and economize in that way. Many pantry ingredients are fundamentally economical too—pasta, rice, and grains are tasty and cheap, and fantastic for filling up hungry families. And ingredients such as canned tuna and sardines can be cheaper than fresh and have the added advantage of a long shelf life, so you're not restricted as to when you have to use them up. Canned vegetables such as tomatoes and corn are also inexpensive and versatile, and invaluable for cooking up a cheap meal in a matter of minutes.

Choose the basics

Make sure that you've got a wide variety of carbohydrates to serve with your meals, or to make meals with. Noodles, pasta (both long strands and short shapes), rice, and couscous all make good choices because they've got a long shelf life and are incredibly versatile. Try them in dishes such as Mixed Bean Kedgeree, page 114, Pasta Pie, page 118, Pasta with Tomato & Basil Sauce, page 110, or Teriyaki Chicken served with egg noodles, page 152. Canned ingredients are essential in every pantry and, in addition to the vegetables mentioned above, beans and legumes, canned fruit such as apricots and pineapple, tuna, and coconut milk are all indispensable. Other dried essentials include herbs and spices, salt and pepper, and flour

and sugar. Oil (olive and a flavorless oil such as vegetable or sunflower) together with vinegar and other condiments such as mustard, vinegar, and soy sauce are also vital pantry supplies, central to cooking and flavoring countless dishes from salads and stir-fries to soups and stews.

Check out the bulk buys

Most supermarkets have offers every week for fantastic bulk buys that seem to provide great value for money, but always stop and think before you pile these bargains into your cart. Will you be able to use up what you're buying? If you can't, then you're wasting food and money, so this cheap deal may not be quite as advantageous as it appears. A giant can of baked beans isn't a bargain if you can only use up half of it,

but three cans of tomatoes for the price of two that you can keep in the pantry might well be worth buying.

Check out the price

Often buying in larger quantities is cheaper, and most supermarkets show not only the pack price but the unit price too, so you can see if what you're buying is a bargain per ounce or per pound. For ingredients such as pasta or rice that you frequently use, it's usually more economical to buy one large packet to keep in the pantry rather than two smaller ones.

Check out the shelf life

Some dry ingredients such as dried herbs and ground spices have a relatively short shelf life and lose their flavor after a time, so unless you use them very regularly you might be better off buying them in smaller

amounts. Similarly, nuts and oils can turn rancid over time, so it's important to buy in quantities that you will use before the use-by date is up.

Fantastic freezing

The home freezer can be an absolute boon to the budget cook and can also be a real time-saver. You can buy ready-frozen ingredients from the supermarket to store in your freezer, or you can freeze your own ingredients such as fruit and vegetables at home. Either freeze them as plain ingredients, or cook them up in soups, sauces, casseroles, or desserts that freeze well, so you've got ready-prepared, homemade meals available in the freezer.

Because freezer items have a long shelf life, you can buy ingredients in bulk, which can often prove cheaper. You can buy big bags of vegetables or shrimp, for example, and just throw a handful into dishes as required. However, foods can't be frozen indefinitely and most should be used up within around three months, so always check the label and don't buy more than you know you can use up. If you freeze your own produce, always label it with the date of freezing.

Choose quality ingredients

Some ingredients such as peas and corn are often better frozen than fresh. The natural sugars in these vegetables start to turn to

dishes in the minimum of time that will out-shine their ready-made commercial counterparts in taste and undercut them in cost. Fresh stock, for instance, makes for perfect homemade soups and risottos, such as Tomato Risoni Soup, page 32, and Carrot, Pea, & Fava Bean Risotto, page 104, while frozen pastry—both puff and shortcrust—can be used to create such delicious delights as Caramelized Banana Puff Tart, page 218, Apricot Tartlets, page 204, and Strawberry & Blueberry Tartlets, page 234.

Seasonal bargains

Frozen ingredients can often prove a better choice when fresh ones are out of season. And when the fresh ingredients are in season why not buy them in bulk when they're cheap and in abundance and freeze them yourself at home? Berries, for example, are easy to freeze, and it means you can enjoy them at summer prices long after summer is over.

Grow your own

If you grow your own fruit and vegetables, you can often end up with gluts of produce, so rather than wasting these valuable ingredients why not freeze them?

Take advantage of offers

Save money with bulk-buy offers and store what you don't need in the freezer for a later date.

starch as soon as they are picked, so unless you can be sure of a really fresh source you'll often get better-quality ingredients by buying the frozen variety because they are processed so soon after harvesting.

Save time and money

Because most ingredients such as fruit, vegetables, meat, poultry, and fish are prepared before freezing, it can save you time in the kitchen, and time often means money! Although you might need to remember to allow time for your chicken to thaw out before cooking, transferring some chicken pieces from the freezer to the refrigerator is easier than jointing a whole chicken. It's also worth keeping a supply of quality time-saving ingredients ready in the freezer so that you can make upmarket

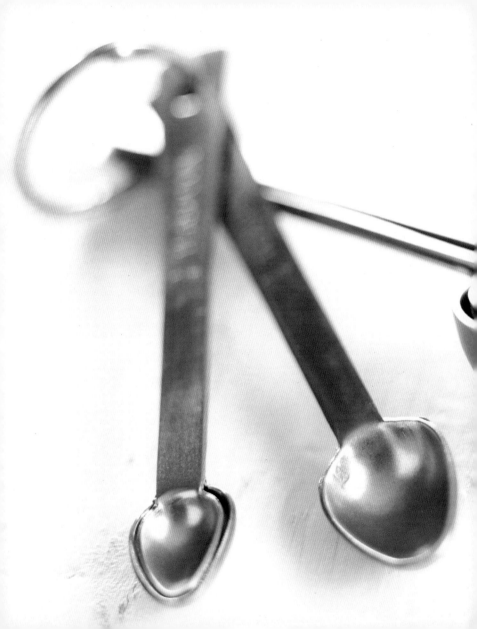

appetizers & snacks

Camembert "fondue"

Serves **4**

Preparation time **10 minutes**

Cooking time **5–10 minutes**

1 whole **Camembert cheese**,
  8 oz in weight

2 tablespoons **olive oil**

leaves stripped from
  2 **rosemary sprigs**

crusty **French bread**

½ cup **walnuts**, roughly
  chopped and toasted

2 tablespoons **honey**

Put the Camembert in an ovenproof dish. Make a few cuts in the top, then drizzle with the oil and sprinkle with the rosemary leaves.

Cover with foil and bake in a preheated oven, 400°F, for 5–10 minutes until gooey.

Cut the French bread into chunky pieces and lightly toast until golden brown.

Sprinkle the walnuts over the cooked Camembert, drizzle with the honey, and serve immediately with the toasted chunks of bread.

For Brie & hazelnut "fondue", use an 8 oz round of Brie instead of the Camembert and sprinkle ⅓ cup hazelnuts, toasted and chopped, over the baked cheese in place of the walnuts.

tomato & mozzarella tartlets

Serves **6**
Preparation time **20 minutes**
Cooking time **20 minutes**

8 oz **puff pastry**, defrosted
if frozen
6 tablespoons **sundried
tomato paste**
3 **plum tomatoes**, seeded
and roughly chopped
4 oz **mozzarella cheese**,
roughly diced
8 **pitted black olives**, roughly
chopped
1 **garlic clove**, finely chopped
2 tablespoons roughly
chopped **oregano**
1 tablespoon **pine nuts**
olive oil, for drizzling
salt and pepper

Line a large baking sheet with nonstick parchment paper. Roll out the pastry on a lightly floured work surface to ⅛ inch thick. Use a 5 inch round cutter to stamp out 6 rounds and lay on the prepared baking sheet.

Spread 1 tablespoon sundried tomato paste over each pastry round. In a small bowl, mix together the tomatoes, mozzarella, olives, garlic, oregano, and pine nuts and season well with salt and pepper. Divide the mixture between the pastry rounds.

Drizzle a little olive oil over the tartlets and bake in a preheated oven, 400°F, for 20 minutes or until the pastry is golden. Serve immediately with mixed salad leaves.

For tomato & anchovy tartlets, follow the first stage of the recipe, then spread 1 tablespoon pesto over each pastry round instead of the sundried tomato paste. In a bowl, mix the tomatoes, olives, and garlic, as above, with a 2 oz can anchovy fillets in oil, drained and snipped into small pieces, ⅓ cup drained and chopped bottled roasted red peppers in oil, and 2 tablespoons chopped basil and season well with salt and pepper. Divide between the pastry rounds, drizzle with olive oil, and bake as above.

goat cheese & chive soufflés

Serves **4**
Preparation time **10 minutes**
Cooking time **20–25 minutes**

2 tablespoons **unsalted butter**
2 tablespoons **all-purpose flour**
1 cup **milk**
4 oz **soft goat cheese**
3 **eggs**, separated
2 tablespoons chopped **chives**
salt and pepper

Melt the butter in a saucepan, add the flour, and cook over a low heat, stirring, for 30 seconds. Remove the pan from the heat and gradually stir in the milk until smooth. Return to the heat and cook, stirring constantly, until the mixture thickens. Cook for 1 minute.

Allow to cool slightly, then beat in the goat cheese, egg yolks, chives, and salt and pepper to taste.

Beat the egg whites in a large, perfectly clean bowl, until soft peaks form. Fold the egg whites into the cheese mixture. Spoon the mixture into 4 greased, individual soufflé ramekins and set on a baking sheet. Bake in a preheated oven, 400°F, for 15–18 minutes until risen and golden. Serve immediately.

For cheddar & chili soufflés, use 1 cup grated cheddar cheese instead of soft goat cheese and 2 tablespoons finely chopped cilantro leaves in place of the chives, and also beat 2 finely chopped red chilies, seeded according to taste, into the egg yolk mixture.

potato & bacon cakes

Serves **4**
Preparation time **15 minutes**,
  plus chilling
Cooking time **about**
  45 minutes

2 lb **potatoes**, cut into chunks
vegetable oil, for pan-frying
6 **scallions**, sliced
7 oz **Canadian bacon**,
  chopped
2 tablespoons chopped
  flat-leaf parsley
all-purpose flour, for coating
2 tablespoons **butter**
salt and pepper

For the tomato sauce
¾ cup **plain yogurt**
2 tablespoons chopped **basil**
2 tablespoons chopped
  tomatoes

Cook the potatoes in a large saucepan of salted boiling water for 15–20 minutes until tender. Drain well, return to the pan, and mash.

Heat a little oil in a skillet, add the scallions, and cook for 2–3 minutes, then add the bacon and cook until browned. Add to the mash with the parsley. Season well with salt and pepper. Form the potato mixture into 8 cakes, then cover and chill in the refrigerator until firm.

Lightly coat the cakes in flour. Melt the butter in a nonstick skillet, add the cakes, in batches, and cook over a medium heat for 4–5 minutes on each side until browned and heated through.

Meanwhile, to make the sauce, put the yogurt in a bowl and mix in the basil and tomatoes. Season well with salt and pepper.

Serve the cakes hot with the sauce.

For salmon fishcakes with sour cream & mushroom sauce, use a 7 oz can red salmon instead of the bacon. Drain and flake the salmon into the mashed potato mixture. Form into cakes and cook as above. Meanwhile, melt 2 tablespoons butter in a saucepan, add 1½ cups sliced button mushrooms and cook for 1 minute. Stir in ¾ cup sour cream and ¼ teaspoon paprika and season to taste with salt and pepper. Heat through gently and serve with the fishcakes.

eggplant, tomato, & feta rolls

Serves **4**
Preparation time **15 minutes**
Cooking time **about
  6 minutes**

2 **eggplants**
3 tablespoons **olive oil**
4 oz **feta cheese**, roughly
  diced
12 **sundried tomatoes in oil**,
  drained
15–20 **basil leaves**
salt and pepper

Trim the ends of the eggplants, then cut a thin slice lengthwise from either side of each; discard these slices, which should be mainly skin. Cut each eggplant lengthwise into 4 slices. Heat the broiler on the hottest setting or heat a griddle pan until very hot.

Brush both sides of the eggplant slices with the oil, then cook under the broiler or in the griddle pan for 3 minutes on each side or until browned and softened.

Lay the eggplant slices on a board and divide the feta, tomatoes, and basil leaves between them. Season well with salt and pepper. Roll up each slice from a short end and secure with a toothpick. Arrange on serving plates and serve immediately, or cover and set aside in a cool place, but not the refrigerator, and serve at room temperature when required.

For zucchini & mozzarella rolls, use 3–4 large zucchini, then trim the ends and sides as for the eggplants. Cut each zucchini lengthwise into 3 slices, depending on their thickness, brush with oil, and cook under the broiler or in a griddle pan as for the eggplants until browned and softened. Spread the zucchini slices with red pesto, then top with 4 oz diced mozzarella cheese and the basil leaves. Roll up and serve as above.

mixed bean salsa with tortilla chips

Serves **4**

Preparation time **10 minutes**,
  plus standing

2 x 13 oz cans **mixed beans**,
  drained and rinsed
3 **tomatoes**, chopped
1 **red bell pepper**, cored,
  seeded, and finely diced
6 **scallions**, sliced
1 teaspoon finely chopped
  red chili
2 tablespoons **olive oil**
1 tablespoon **white wine**
  vinegar
chopped **cilantro**, to garnish
salt and pepper

To serve
tortilla chips
sour cream

Put the beans, tomatoes, red pepper, and scallions in a food processor and blend until fairly smooth.

In a small bowl, beat together the chili, oil, and vinegar, pour over the bean mixture and toss to coat. Season to taste with salt and pepper and garnish with cilantro. Cover and allow to stand at room temperature for about 30 minutes to allow the flavors to mingle.

Serve the salsa with tortilla chips and sour cream.

For mixed bean pilau, which will work as a substantial appetizer or side dish, add 2 cups basmati rice to a pan, cover with 2½ cups water and bring to a boil. Reduce the heat, cover, and simmer for 12 minutes without removing the lid. Remove from the heat, toss in the mixed bean salsa (see above), and stir in 3 tablespoons chopped cilantro leaves. Replace the lid and return to a very low heat for 5 minutes. Serve hot.

onion & mushroom quesadillas

Serves **4**
Preparation time **10 minutes**
Cooking time **about
30 minutes**

3 tablespoons **olive oil**
2 **red onions**, thinly sliced
1 teaspoon **superfine sugar**
8 **flour tortillas**
3 cups sliced **button
mushrooms**
1⅛ cups grated **cheddar
cheese**
1 small handful of **parsley**,
chopped
salt and pepper

Heat 2 tablespoons of the oil in a large skillet, add the
onions, and cook until soft. Add the sugar and cook for
3 minutes or until caramelized. Remove the onions with
a slotted spoon and set aside. Heat the remaining oil in
the pan, add the mushrooms, and cook for 3 minutes
or until golden brown. Set aside.

Heat a nonstick skillet and add 1 tortilla. Sprinkle with
a quarter of the red onions, mushrooms, cheddar, and
parsley. Season to taste with salt and pepper. Cover
with another tortilla and cook until browned on the
underside. Turn over and cook until browned on the
other side. Remove from the pan and keep warm.

Repeat with the remaining tortillas and ingredients.
Cut into wedges and serve with a salad.

For spinach & Brie quesadillas, replace the
mushrooms with 1 cup cooked, chopped spinach
leaves and use 5 oz Brie, cut into slices, instead of
the cheddar. Cook and serve as above.

fried goat cheese

Serves **4**
Preparation time **15 minutes**
Cooking time **10 minutes**

4 individual **goat cheeses**,
   about 2½ oz each
2 **eggs**, beaten
4 tablespoons **fresh white
   bread crumbs**
about ¾ cup **vegetable oil**,
   for deep-frying
2½ cups **arugula leaves**
2 tablespoons **olive oil**
salt and pepper

For red onion marmalade
1 tablespoon **olive oil**
2 **red onions**, thinly sliced
½ cup **red wine**
3 tablespoons **red wine
   vinegar**
¼ cup **superfine sugar**

Dip the cheeses in the beaten egg and then coat evenly with the bread crumbs. Cover and chill while you prepare the onion marmalade.

Heat the olive oil in a small saucepan, add the onions, and cook for 2 minutes. Stir in the wine, vinegar, and sugar, then cook for 5 minutes or until the onions are translucent. Remove with a slotted spoon and set aside, reserving the juices in the pan.

Heat the vegetable oil in a nonstick skillet to 350–375°F or until a cube of bread browns in 30 seconds. (Take care not to overfill the pan. If necessary, use a saucepan or deep skillet.) Add the goat cheeses and cook for 2 minutes or until golden. Remove with a slotted spoon and drain well on paper towels.

Divide the arugula between 4 plates and drizzle the olive oil and reserved juices from the onions over the top. Season to taste with salt and pepper. Place the goat cheeses on the arugula and top with the onion marmalade. Serve immediately.

For fried Camembert & tomato-chili sauce, cut an 8 oz Camembert into wedges, coat, and chill as above. Bring a 13 oz can chopped tomatoes, 2–3 finely chopped red chilies, 2 crushed garlic cloves, ½ cup light brown sugar, 4 tablespoons white wine vinegar, 1 tablespoon Worcestershire sauce, and ½ teaspoon salt to a boil in a saucepan. Reduce the heat and simmer gently for 30 minutes or until thick. Cook the Camembert as above and serve with the sauce.

tomato risoni soup

Serves **4**
Preparation time **10 minutes**
Cooking time **18 minutes**

2 tablespoons **olive oil**, plus
  extra for drizzling
1 large **onion**, finely chopped
2 **celery sticks**, finely
  chopped
4 **large tomatoes**
6 cups **vegetable stock**
5 oz **dried risoni or orzo** or
  any tiny shaped dried pasta
6 tablespoons finely chopped
  flat-leaf parsley
salt and pepper

Heat the oil in a large saucepan over a medium heat, add the onion and celery, and cook until soft.

Meanwhile, score a cross in the base of each tomato, then put in a heatproof bowl of boiling water for 1 minute. Plunge into cold water, then peel the skin away from the cross. Halve the tomatoes, then scoop out the seeds and discard. Roughly chop the flesh.

Add the tomatoes, stock, onions, and celery to the pan and bring to a boil. Add the pasta and cook for 10 minutes or until al dente. Season to taste with salt and pepper and stir in the parsley.

Remove from the heat, ladle into warmed bowls, and drizzle with oil before serving.

For homemade vegetable stock, put 1¼ lb mixed vegetables (excluding potatoes, parsnips, and other starchy root vegetables), 2 peeled garlic cloves, 8 peppercorns, and 1 bouquet garni in a large saucepan, add 7 cups water and bring to a boil. Reduce the heat and simmer gently for 40 minutes, skimming any scum that rises to the surface. Strain through a cheesecloth-lined sieve. If not using straight away, allow to cool before covering and refrigerating.

corn & pepper frittata

Serves **4**
Preparation time **10 minutes**
Cooking time **about
10 minutes**

2 tablespoons **olive oil**
4 **scallions**, thinly sliced
7 oz can **corn**, drained
5 oz bottled **roasted red
sweet peppers** in oil,
drained and cut into strips
4 **eggs**, lightly beaten
1 cup grated **strong cheddar
cheese**
1 small handful of **chives**,
finely chopped
salt and pepper

Heat the oil in a skillet, add the scallions, corn, and red peppers and cook for 30 seconds.

Add the eggs, cheddar, chives, and salt and pepper to taste and cook over a medium heat for 4–5 minutes until the base is set. Remove from the burner, place under a preheated broiler, and cook for 3–4 minutes or until golden and set. Cut into wedges and serve immediately with a green salad and crusty bread.

For zucchini, pepper, & Gruyère frittata, use 1 cup finely chopped zucchini instead of the corn, 1 cup grated Gruyère cheese in place of the cheddar and substitute 4 tablespoons chopped mint leaves for the chives.

smoked trout bruschetta

Serves **4**
Preparation time **5 minutes**
Cooking time **5 minutes**

12 thick slices of **French bread**
2 **large garlic cloves**, halved
2 tablespoons **extra virgin olive oil**, plus extra for drizzling
½ cup **tzatziki**
8 oz **hot smoked trout**, flaked
chopped **dill weed**, to garnish
pepper

Toast the bread in a preheated griddle pan or under a preheated broiler.

While still hot, rub the toast all over with the garlic halves and sprinkle with the oil. Top each piece with a large spoonful of tzatziki and pile on the trout. Season to taste with pepper and serve garnished with chopped dill weed and drizzled with extra oil.

For homemade tzatziki, coarsely grate 1 large cucumber and squeeze out all the liquid, then put the flesh in a bowl. Add 4–5 tablespoons thick Greek or whole milk yogurt, season well with salt and pepper, and mix together.

smoked salmon cones

Serves **4**

Preparation time **15 minutes**

2 **small cucumbers**, halved
lengthwise, seeded, and cut
into thin strips

1 teaspoon prepared **English
mustard**

1 tablespoon **white wine
vinegar**

½ teaspoon **superfine sugar**

1 tablespoon finely
chopped **dill weed**

2 **flour tortillas**

4 tablespoons **sour cream**

4 oz **smoked salmon
trimmings**, any larger pieces
cut into wide strips

salt and pepper

Put the cucumber strips in a shallow glass or ceramic
bowl. In a small bowl, mix together the mustard,
vinegar, sugar, and dill weed. Season well with salt and
pepper, then pour over the cucumbers. Allow to stand
for 5 minutes.

Cut the tortillas in half and lay on a board or work
surface. Spread 1 tablespoon sour cream over each
tortilla half.

Divide the smoked salmon pieces between the tortillas
and top with the cucumber mixture. Add a little salt and
pepper, if desired, and roll up each tortilla to form a
cone around the filling. Secure each cone with a
toothpick, if desired.

For chicken & mango cones, put 4 oz diced, cooked
chicken breast meat, 1 large peeled, pitted, and diced
mango, and 1 tablespoon chopped cilantro leaves in a
bowl. Add 4 tablespoons mayonnaise, a squeeze of
lime juice, and salt and pepper to taste. Toss gently to
combine, then divide between the tortilla halves and
roll up, as above.

risi e bisi

Serves **4**

Preparation time **5 minutes**

Cooking time **about 25 minutes**

1 tablespoon **butter**

1 tablespoon **olive oil**

1 **onion**, finely chopped

2 **garlic cloves**, crushed

1¼ cups **risotto rice**

3¾ cups **hot chicken stock**, made with 1 chicken bouillon cube and boiling water, heated to simmering

3 cups **frozen peas**

¼ cup grated **Parmesan cheese**

4 oz **cooked ham**, finely chopped

1 bunch of **parsley**, finely chopped

salt and pepper

Melt the butter with the oil in a saucepan, add the onion and garlic, and cook until the onion is soft and starting to brown. Add the rice and stir until coated with the butter mixture.

Add the hot stock, a ladleful at a time, and cook, stirring constantly, until each addition has been absorbed before adding the next. Continue until all the stock has been absorbed and the rice is creamy and cooked but still retains a little bite—this will take around 15 minutes.

Add the peas and heat through for 3–5 minutes. Remove from the heat and stir in the Parmesan, ham, and parsley. Season to taste with salt and pepper and serve immediately.

For tuna & tomato risotto, after cooking the onion and garlic, add 3 tablespoons white wine and cook, stirring, until it has evaporated. Then follow the recipe above, but use fish stock instead of chicken stock and add 2 chopped tomatoes in place of the peas, along with a 7 oz can tuna, drained and flaked, and heat through for 3–5 minutes. Remove from the heat and stir in 2 tablespoons chopped basil leaves with the Parmesan cheese and salt and pepper to taste. Serve immediately.

minted pea soup

Serves **4**
Preparation time **10 minutes**
Cooking time **20 minutes**

1 tablespoon **butter**
1 **onion**, finely chopped
1 **potato**, finely chopped
4 cups **vegetable stock**
2½ cups **frozen peas**
6 tablespoons finely chopped
  mint leaves
salt and pepper
crème fraîche or **sour cream**
  (optional), to serve

Melt the butter in a saucepan, add the onion and potato, and cook for 5 minutes. Add the stock and bring to a boil, then reduce heat and simmer gently for 10 minutes or until the potato is tender.

Add the peas to the pan and cook for an additional 3–4 minutes. Season well with salt and pepper, remove from the heat and stir in the mint. Puree in a food processor or blender until smooth. Ladle into warmed bowls and top each with a dollop of crème fraîche or soure cream, if desired.

For chunky pea & ham soup, cook 1 chopped carrot and 1 chopped turnip with the onion and potato, then add 4 cups ham or chicken stock. Once the root vegetables are tender, add 10 oz chopped cooked ham, 4 finely chopped scallions, and 2 tablespoons chopped parsley with the peas and cook for 3–4 minutes. Do not blend the soup, but ladle into warmed bowls and serve with crusty bread.

goat cheese & tomato tarts

Serves **4**
Preparation time **15 minutes**
Cooking time **10–12 minutes**

4 sheets of **phyllo pastry**,
  about 10 inches square each
1 tablespoon **olive oil**
20 **cherry tomatoes**, halved
7 oz **firm goat cheese**, cut
  into ½ inch cubes
2 tablespoons **pine nuts**
2 teaspoons **thyme leaves**
salt and pepper

Lightly oil 4 individual tartlet pans, each about 4 inches in diameter. Brush a sheet of phyllo pastry with a little of the oil. Cut in half, then across into 4 equal-size squares and use to line one of the pans. Repeat with the remaining pastry sheets. Brush any remaining oil over the pastry in the pans.

Put 5 tomato halves in the bottom of each tartlet. Top with the goat cheese, then add the remaining tomato halves and pine nuts. Sprinkle with the thyme leaves and season well with salt and pepper.

Bake the tartlets in a preheated oven, 400°F, for 10–12 minutes or until the pastry is crisp and golden. Serve hot with a leafy green salad.

For feta & pepper tarts, roll out 6 oz puff pastry on a lightly floured work surface and use to line the tartlet pans. Core and seed 1 yellow and 1 orange bell pepper, then slice into thin strips and toss in a little olive oil. Cut 7 oz feta cheese into ½ inch cubes. Divide half the pepper strips between the tartlets, top with the cheese, then add the remaining pepper strips, and sprinkle with the pine nuts, as above. Sprinkle with 2 teaspoons dried oregano and season well with salt and pepper. Bake at the same temperature as specified above for about 15 minutes or until the pastry is golden.

vegetable & salad dishes

spinach & potato gratin

Serves **4**
Preparation time **10 minutes**
Cooking time **35 minutes**

1¼ lb **potatoes**, thinly sliced
1 lb **spinach leaves**
7 oz **mozzarella cheese**,
   grated
4 **tomatoes**, sliced
3 **eggs**, beaten
1¼ cups **whipping cream**
salt and pepper

Cook the potato slices in a large saucepan of salted boiling water for 5 minutes, then drain well.

Meanwhile, cook the spinach in a separate saucepan of boiling water for 1–2 minutes. Drain and squeeze out the excess water.

Grease a large ovenproof dish and line the bottom with half the potato slices. Cover with the spinach and half the mozzarella, seasoning each layer well with salt and pepper. Cover with the remaining potato slices and arrange the tomato slices on top. Sprinkle with the remaining mozzarella.

Beat the eggs and cream together in a bowl and season well with salt and pepper. Pour over the ingredients in the dish.

Bake in a preheated oven, 350°F, for about 30 minutes. Serve immediately with a salad and crusty bread.

For tomato, lime, & basil salad to serve as an accompaniment, slice or quarter 2 lb tomatoes while the gratin is baking, and arrange in a large serving bowl. Sprinkle with ½ red onion, thinly sliced, and 1 handful of basil leaves. Beat together 4 tablespoons olive oil, 2 tablespoons chopped basil, 1 tablespoon lime juice, 1 teaspoon grated lime zest, ½ teaspoon honey, 1 crushed garlic clove, a pinch of cayenne pepper, and salt and pepper to taste. Pour over the salad. Cover and let stand at room temperature for about 30 minutes to allow the flavors to mingle, then serve with the gratin.

mushroom stroganoff

Serves **4**
Preparation time **10 minutes**
Cooking time **10 minutes**

1 tablespoon **butter**
2 tablespoons **olive oil**
1 **onion**, thinly sliced
4 **garlic cloves**, finely
  chopped
1 lb **chestnut mushrooms**,
  sliced
2 tablespoons **wholegrain
  mustard**
1 cup **sour cream**
salt and pepper
3 tablespoons chopped
  parsley, to garnish

Melt the butter with the oil in a large skillet, add the onion and garlic, and cook until soft and starting to brown.

Add the mushrooms to the pan and cook until soft and starting to brown. Stir in the mustard and sour cream and just heat through. Season to taste with salt and pepper, then serve immediately, garnished with the chopped parsley.

For mushroom soup with garlic croutons, while the mushrooms are cooking, remove the crusts from 2 thick slices of day-old white bread and rub with 2 halved garlic cloves. Cut the bread into cubes. Fry the cubes of bread in a shallow depth of vegetable oil in a skillet, turning constantly, for 5 minutes or until browned all over and crisp. Drain on paper towels. After adding the mustard and sour cream to the mushroom mixture as above, add 1¾ cups boiling hot vegetable stock, then puree the mixture in a food processor or blender until smooth. Serve in warmed bowls, topped with the croutons and garnished with the chopped parsley.

greek vegetable casserole

Serves **4**
Preparation time **10 minutes**
Cooking time **25 minutes**

4 tablespoons **olive oil**
1 **onion**, thinly sliced
3 bell **peppers** of mixed
    colors, cored, seeded,
    and sliced into rings
4 **garlic cloves**, crushed
4 **tomatoes**, chopped
7 oz **feta cheese**, cubed
1 teaspoon **dried oregano**
salt and pepper
chopped **flat-leaf parsley**,
    to garnish

Heat 3 tablespoons of the oil in a flameproof casserole, add the onion, peppers, and garlic, and cook until soft and starting to brown. Add the tomatoes and cook for a few minutes until softened. Mix in the feta and oregano, season to taste with salt and pepper, and drizzle with the remaining oil.

Cover and cook in a preheated oven, 400°F, for 15 minutes. Garnish with the parsley and serve with warmed crusty bread.

For Middle Eastern vegetable casserole, heat 1 tablespoon olive oil in a flameproof casserole, add 1 red onion, cut into wedges, 3 sliced celery sticks, and 3 thinly sliced carrots and cook until soft and starting to brown. Add 2 teaspoons harissa and cook, stirring, for 1 minute. Add about 1¼ lb eggplants, trimmed and chopped, 2 large chopped tomatoes, and 1 cup water. Bring to a boil, then cover and cook in a preheated oven, 350°F, for about 25 minutes. Stir in 2 large potatoes, peeled and thickly sliced, and cook for an additional 15 minutes or until tender but still firm. Serve hot garnished with chopped cilantro.

golden mushroom & leek pies

Serves **4**
Preparation time **15 minutes**
Cooking time **25–30 minutes**

2 tablespoons **butter**
2 **leeks**, thinly sliced
10 oz **chestnut mushrooms**, quartered
10 oz **button mushrooms**, quartered
1 tablespoon **all-purpose flour**
1 cup **milk**
⅔ cup **heavy cream**
1 cup grated **strong cheddar cheese**
4 tablespoons finely chopped **parsley**
2 sheets of **ready-rolled puff pastry**, defrosted if frozen
1 **egg**, beaten

Melt the butter in a large saucepan, add the leeks, and cook for 1–2 minutes. Add the mushrooms and cook for 2 minutes. Stir in the flour and cook, stirring, for 1 minute, then gradually add the milk and cream and cook, stirring constantly, until the mixture thickens. Add the cheddar and the parsley and cook, stirring, for 1–2 minutes. Remove from the heat.

Cut 4 rounds from the pastry sheets to cover 4 individual pie dishes. Divide the mushroom mixture between the pie dishes. Brush the rims with the beaten egg, then place the pastry rounds on top. Press down around the rims and crimp the edges with a fork. Cut a couple of slits in the top of each pie to let the steam out. Brush the pastry with the remaining egg.

Bake in a preheated oven, 425°F, for 15–20 minutes until the pastry is golden brown. Serve immediately.

For curried ham & mushroom pies, follow the first stage above, but after cooking the mushrooms add 1 teaspoon medium curry powder and ½ teaspoon turmeric to the pan and cook, stirring, for 1 minute, before adding the flour and continuing with the recipe. Once the sauce has thickened, stir in 7 oz cooked ham, cut into small bite-size pieces, in place of the cheddar and 4 tablespoons chopped cilantro leaves instead of the parsley. Make and bake the pies as above.

stuffed mushrooms with tofu

Serves **1**
Preparation time **15 minutes**
Cooking time **20 minutes**

1¼ cups **boiling water**
1 teaspoon **organic
vegetable bouillon powder**
2 large **portobello
mushrooms**, stalks removed
1 tablespoon **olive oil**
3 tablespoons finely chopped
red onion
4 oz **firm tofu**, diced
1 tablespoon **pine nuts**,
toasted
¼ teaspoon **cayenne pepper**
1 tablespoon **chopped basil**
¼ cup finely grated **Parmesan
cheese**
2 cups **baby spinach leaves**
salt and pepper

Pour the boiling water into a wide pan, then stir in the
bouillon powder. Add the mushrooms and poach for
2–3 minutes, then remove with a slotted spoon and
drain on paper towels.

Heat a little of the oil in a pan, add the onion, and cook
until soft. Remove from the heat and let cool.

Mix together the onion, tofu, pine nuts, cayenne
pepper, basil, and the remaining oil. Season well with
salt and pepper.

Sprinkle some Parmesan over each mushroom, then
stuff the mushrooms with the onion mixture. Arrange
in a flameproof dish and cook about 6 inches below
a preheated medium broiler for 10 minutes or until
heated through and the cheese has melted.

To serve, sprinkle the spinach leaves on a plate and
arrange the hot mushrooms on top.

For baba ghanoush, a Middle Eastern eggplant dip
that makes a great accompaniment to this dish, prick
1 eggplant all over with a fork, cut lengthwise in half,
then lay, cut-side down, on a greased baking sheet.
Bake in a preheated oven, 375°F, for 30–40 minutes
until softened. When cool enough to handle, peel,
then puree in a food processor or blender with
½ crushed garlic clove and 1 teaspoon lemon juice.
With the motor still running, gradually trickle in
1 tablespoon olive oil to make a creamy paste. Stir
in 1 tablespoon chopped parsley and season to taste
with salt and pepper. Add a generous dollop on the
side of the mushrooms.

mushrooms à la grecque

Serves **4**

Preparation time **10 minutes**,
  plus standing

Cooking time **10 minutes**

8 tablespoons **olive oil**

2 **large onions**, sliced

3 **garlic cloves**, finely
  chopped

1¼ lb **button mushrooms**,
  halved

8 **plum tomatoes**, roughly
  chopped or 13 oz can
  chopped tomatoes

½ cup **pitted black olives**

2 tablespoons **white wine
  vinegar**

salt and pepper

chopped **parsley**, to garnish

Heat 2 tablespoons of the oil in a large skillet, add the onions and garlic, and cook until soft and starting to brown. Add the mushrooms and tomatoes and cook, stirring gently, for 4–5 minutes. Remove from the heat.

Transfer the mushroom mixture to a serving dish and garnish with the olives.

Beat the remaining oil with the vinegar in a small bowl, season to taste with salt and pepper, and drizzle over the salad. Garnish with the chopped parsley, cover, and let stand at room temperature for 30 minutes to allow the flavors to mingle before serving.

For mushroom pasta salad, prepare the mushroom mixture as above. Cook 7 oz dried pennette or farfalle in a large saucepan of salted boiling water according to the package instructions until al dente. Meanwhile, cook 4 oz green beans in a saucepan of salted boiling water until just tender. Drain the beans, refresh under cold running water, and drain again. Drain the pasta thoroughly and toss into the mushroom mixture with the beans and 2 tablespoons torn basil leaves. Serve at room temperature.

broiled endive with salsa verde

Serves **4**
Preparation time **15 minutes**
Cooking time **10 minutes**

4 **heads of Belgian endive**,
  about 5 oz each, trimmed
  and halved lengthwise
2 tablespoons **olive oil**
4 oz **Parmesan cheese**,
  coarsely grated
chopped **parsley**, to garnish

For the salsa verde
4 cups **flat-leaf parsley**
⅓ cup **pine nuts**, toasted
2 **pickled gherkins**
8 **pitted green olives**
1 **garlic clove**, chopped
1 tablespoon **lemon juice**
⅔ cup **olive oil**
salt and pepper

Coarsely puree all the ingredients for the salsa verde, except the oil, in a food processor or blender. With the motor still running, gradually trickle in the oil to make a creamy paste. Transfer to a serving dish, cover, and set aside. (The salsa will keep for up to 1 week in the refrigerator.)

Heat the broiler on the hottest setting. Arrange the endive halves on the broiler rack, cut-sides down, brush with some of the oil, and cook under the broiler for 5 minutes. Turn the endive halves over, brush with the remaining oil, and sprinkle the Parmesan over the top. Cook for an additional 4 minutes or until the cheese has melted and the edges of the endive begin to char.

Transfer the endive to plates and garnish with chopped parsley. Add a little salsa verde to each plate and serve immediately, offering the remaining salsa verde separately. Toasted ciabatta bread is a good accompaniment.

For broiled sardines with salsa verde, arrange 1½ lb whole, cleaned and gutted sardines in a large, shallow, glass or ceramic dish. Beat together 3 tablespoons olive oil, 2 garlic cloves, the grated zest and juice of 1 lemon, and 2 teaspoons dried oregano. Pour over the fish and turn them in the marinade to coat, then cover and allow to marinate in the refrigerator for about 1 hour. Meanwhile, prepare the salsa verde as above. Cook the sardines under a preheated broiler or over a barbecue for 4–5 minutes on each side, basting with the marinade. Serve with the salsa verde.

curried cauliflower with chickpeas

Serves **4**
Preparation time **10 minutes**
Cooking time **20 minutes**

2 tablespoons **olive oil**
1 **onion**, chopped
2 **garlic cloves**, crushed
4 tablespoons **medium
curry paste**
1 **small cauliflower**, divided
into florets
1½ cups **vegetable stock**,
made with 1 vegetable
bouillon cube and boiling
water
4 **tomatoes**, roughly chopped
13 oz canned **chickpeas**,
drained and rinsed
2 tablespoons **mango
chutney**
salt and pepper
4 tablespoons chopped
cilantro, to garnish
beaten **plain yogurt**, to serve
(optional)

Heat the oil in a saucepan, add the onion and garlic
and cook until the onion is soft and starting to brown.
Stir in the curry paste, add the cauliflower and stock,
and bring to a boil. Reduce the heat, cover tightly, and
simmer for 10 minutes.

Add the tomatoes, chickpeas, and chutney and
continue to cook, uncovered, for 10 minutes. Season
to taste with salt and pepper. Serve garnished with
cilantro and drizzled with a little beaten yogurt,
if desired.

For homemade mango chutney, put the peeled,
pitted, and sliced flesh of 6 ripe mangoes in a large
saucepan with 1¼ cups white wine vinegar and cook
over a low heat for 10 minutes. Add 1 cup dark brown
sugar, 2 inch piece fresh ginger root, peeled and finely
chopped, 2 crushed garlic cloves, 2 teaspoons chili
powder, and 1 teaspoon salt and bring to a boil,
stirring constantly. Reduce the heat and simmer for
30 minutes, stirring occasionally. Ladle into a sterilized
screw-top jar and replace the lid. Store in the
refrigerator and use within 1 month.

quick one-pot ratatouille

Serves **4**
Preparation time **10 minutes**
Cooking time **20 minutes**

6 tablespoons **olive oil**
2 **onions**, chopped
1 medium **eggplant**, cut
    into bite-size cubes
2 large **zucchini**, cut into
    bite-size pieces
1 **red bell pepper**, cored,
    seeded, and cut into
    bite-size pieces
1 **yellow bell pepper**, cored,
    seeded, and cut into
    bite-size pieces
2 **garlic cloves**, crushed
13 oz can **chopped tomatoes**
4 tablespoons chopped
    parsley or **basil**
salt and pepper

Heat the oil in a large saucepan until very hot, add
the onions, eggplant, zucchini, peppers, and garlic
and cook, stirring constantly, for a few minutes until
softened. Add the tomatoes, season to taste with salt
and pepper, and stir well.

Reduce the heat, cover the pan tightly, and simmer
for 15 minutes until all the vegetables are cooked.
Remove from the heat and stir in the chopped parsley
or basil before serving.

For Mediterranean vegetable pie, spoon the cooked
vegetable mixture into a medium-size ovenproof dish.
Cook 1 lb 10 oz quartered potatoes in a large saucepan
of salted boiling water for 12–15 minutes or until tender,
then drain and roughly mash with 1⅔ cups finely grated
cheddar cheese. Spread over the vegetable mixture,
then bake in a preheated oven, 350°F, for 20 minutes
or until lightly golden on top.

baked eggplants & mozzarella

Serves **4**
Preparation time **10 minutes**
Cooking time **about
25 minutes**

2 **eggplants**, sliced in
  half lengthwise
3 tablespoons **olive oil**
1 **onion**, chopped
1 **garlic clove**, crushed
8 oz can **chopped tomatoes**
1 tablespoon **tomato paste**
10 oz **mozzarella cheese**,
  cut into thin slices
salt and pepper
basil, to garnish

Brush the eggplants with 2 tablespoons of the oil and arrange, cut-side up, on a baking sheet. Roast in a preheated oven, 400°F, for 20 minutes.

Meanwhile, heat the remaining oil in a skillet, add the onion and garlic and cook until the onion is soft and starting to brown. Add the tomatoes and tomato paste and simmer for 5 minutes or until the sauce has thickened.

Remove the eggplants from the oven and cover each half with some sauce and 2 of the mozzarella slices. Season to taste with salt and pepper and return to the oven for 4–5 minutes to melt the cheese. Serve immediately sprinkled with basil leaves.

For roasted garlic bread to serve as an accompaniment, separate 2 garlic bulbs into separate cloves. Put on a square of foil and drizzle generously with olive oil. Bring up the sides of the foil and twist together at the top. Bake in the oven alongside the eggplants, then unwrap and allow to cool slightly before squeezing the flesh from the skins and spreading onto slices of hot French bread. Serve with the baked eggplants.

lebanese lentil & bulghur salad

Serves **4**
Preparation time **10 minutes**
Cooking time **30 minutes**

½ cup **Puy lentils**
1 tablespoon **tomato paste**
3 cups **vegetable stock**
½ cup **bulghur wheat**
juice of **1 lemon**
1 tablespoon **olive oil**
2 **onions**, sliced
1 teaspoon **granulated sugar**
1 bunch of **mint**, chopped
salt and pepper
3 **tomatoes**, finely chopped

Put the lentils, tomato paste, and stock in a saucepan and bring to a boil. Reduce the heat, cover tightly, and simmer for 20 minutes. Add the bulghur wheat and lemon juice and season to taste with salt and pepper. Cook for 10 minutes until all the stock has been absorbed.

Meanwhile, heat the oil in a skillet, add the onions and sugar, and cook over a low heat until deep brown and caramelized.

Stir the mint into the lentil and bulghur wheat mixture, then serve warm, topped with the fried onions and chopped tomato.

For Lebanese-style chicken salad, season 3 chicken breasts with salt and pepper. Brush each one with a little olive oil and place on a very hot griddle pan. Cook for 4–5 minutes on each side or until cooked through and lightly charred on the edges. Cut the breasts into thin slices and stir into the lentil salad above with 1 finely chopped cucumber and 10–12 sliced radishes.

creamy zucchini with walnuts

Serves **4**

Preparation time **10 minutes**

Cooking time **10–15 minutes**

3 tablespoons **olive oil**

1 **onion**, chopped

4 **zucchini**, cut into
  matchsticks

2 **celery sticks**, cut into
  matchsticks

1 cup **cream cheese with
  garlic**

1 cup **walnut pieces**

salt and pepper

Heat the oil in a large skillet, add the onion, and cook for 5 minutes until soft. Add the zucchini and celery and cook for 4–5 minutes until soft and starting to brown.

Add the cheese and cook for 2–3 minutes until melted. Stir in the walnuts, season to taste with salt and pepper, and serve immediately.

For curried zucchini, cook the onion as above, then add 2 small, quartered potatoes and cook for 2–3 minutes. Stir in the zucchini, sliced, with ½ teaspoon chili powder, ½ teaspoon turmeric, 1 teaspoon ground coriander, and ½ teaspoon salt. Add ⅔ cup water, cover, and cook over a low heat for 8–10 minutes until the potatoes are tender.

eggplant & zucchini salad

Serves **4**
Preparation time **15 minutes**
Cooking time **4–6 minutes**

2 **eggplants**, thinly sliced
2 **zucchini**, thinly sliced
3 tablespoons **olive oil**
4 oz **feta cheese**

For the honey-mint dressing
½ cup **mint leaves**, roughly
    chopped, plus extra leaves
    to garnish
1 tablespoon **honey**
1 teaspoon prepared **English
    mustard**
2 tablespoons **lime juice**
salt and pepper

Brush the eggplant and zucchini slices with the oil. Heat the broiler on the hottest setting. Cook the vegetables under the broiler for 2–3 minutes on each side until lightly cooked.

Arrange the broiled vegetables in a shallow dish. Crumble the feta and sprinkle it over the vegetables.

Beat all the dressing ingredients together in a small bowl, seasoning to taste with salt and pepper. Pour the dressing over the salad and toss to coat. Sprinkle with mint leaves to garnish and serve with toasted flat breads or crusty baguette.

For tahini dressing, as an alternative to the honey-mint dressing, put 2 tablespoons tahini paste in a bowl. Slowly beat in 4 tablespoons plain yogurt and 1–2 tablespoons cold water as necessary to make a drizzling consistency. Stir in 2 tablespoons chopped parsley and 1 crushed garlic clove. Season to taste with salt and pepper. Pour over the salad and toss to coat.

thai chicken noodle salad

Serves **4**
Preparation time **10 minutes**
Cooking time **10 minutes**

8 oz **thin rice noodles**
6 tablespoons **Thai sweet chili sauce**
2 tablespoons **Thai fish sauce**
juice of 2 **limes**
2 **cooked boneless, skinless chicken breasts**
1 **cucumber,** cut into ribbons
1 **red chili,** finely chopped
1 small handful of **cilantro leaves**

Put the noodles in a large heatproof bowl and pour boiling water over to cover. Leave for 6–8 minutes until tender, then drain and rinse well under cold running water.

Beat together the sweet chili sauce, fish sauce, and lime juice in a bowl. Shred the chicken and toss with the dressing to coat.

Add the noodles, cucumber, and chili to the chicken mixture and toss gently to combine. Sprinkle with the cilantro leaves and serve immediately.

For seafood noodle salad, replace the chicken with 1 lb cooked peeled shrimp and 7 oz cooked shelled mussels, and sprinkle with a small handful of basil leaves instead of cilantro leaves.

strawberry & cucumber salad

Serves **4–6**

Preparation time **10 minutes**, plus chilling

1 large **cucumber**, halved lengthwise, seeded, and thinly sliced

1⅔ cups **strawberries**, halved or quartered if large

For the balsamic dressing

1 tablespoon **balsamic vinegar**

1 teaspoon **wholegrain mustard**

1 teaspoon **honey**

3 tablespoons **olive oil**

salt and pepper

Put the cucumber slices and strawberry halves or quarters in a shallow bowl.

Put all the dressing ingredients in a screw-top jar, season to taste with salt and pepper, and shake well.

Pour the dressing over the cucumber and strawberries. Toss gently, then cover and chill for 5–10 minutes before serving.

For cucumber & dill salad, prepare the cucumber as specified above, then put the slices in a colander set over a plate or in the sink. Sprinkle with 2 teaspoons salt and let stand for 20–30 minutes, to allow the excess moisture to drain away. Rinse under cold running water, then drain thoroughly and transfer to a shallow serving dish. In a bowl, mix together 4 tablespoons thick Greek or whole milk yogurt, 1 teaspoon white wine vinegar, and 2 tablespoons chopped dill weed. Season well with pepper. Pour over the cucumber, toss gently to combine, and serve garnished with dill sprigs.

chickpea & chili salad

Serves **4**

Preparation time **10 minutes**, plus standing

2 x 13 oz cans **chickpeas**, drained and rinsed

2 **plum tomatoes**, roughly chopped

4 **scallions**, thinly sliced

1 **red chili**, seeded and thinly sliced

4 tablespoons roughly chopped **cilantro leaves**

toasted pita bread, cut into thin fingers, to serve

For the lemon dressing

2 tablespoons **lemon juice**

1 **garlic clove**, crushed

2 tablespoons **olive oil**

salt and pepper

Combine all the salad ingredients in a shallow bowl.

Put all the dressing ingredients in a screw-top jar, season to taste with salt and pepper, and shake well. Pour over the salad and toss well to coat all the ingredients.

Cover the salad and let stand at room temperature for about 10 minutes to allow the flavors to mingle. Serve with toasted pita bread fingers.

For white bean & sundried tomato salad, combine 2 x 13 oz cans cannellini beans, drained and rinsed, 4 oz sundried tomatoes in oil, drained and roughly chopped, 1 tablespoon chopped and pitted black olives, 2 teaspoons drained and rinsed capers, and 2 teaspoons chopped thyme leaves. Toss in the lemon dressing and let stand as above, then serve with toasted slices of ciabatta bread.

chorizo, egg, & ciabatta salad

Serves **4**

Preparation time **10 minutes**

Cooking time **10 minutes**

½ **ciabatta loaf**, cut into chunks

6 tablespoons **olive oil**

2 tablespoons **red wine vinegar**

2 teaspoons **wholegrain mustard**

4 **eggs**

7 oz **chorizo**, thickly sliced

4 handfuls of **young spinach leaves**

salt and pepper

Toss the ciabatta chunks in 2 tablespoons of the oil, spread out on a baking sheet, and bake in a preheated oven, 400°F, for 10 minutes or until golden brown.

Meanwhile, in a small bowl, beat together the remaining oil, the vinegar, and wholegrain mustard to make the dressing.

Poach the eggs in a large saucepan of barely simmering water for 5 minutes. Fry the chorizo in a dry skillet over a medium heat for 3–4 minutes or until crisp and cooked through.

Toss the spinach and chorizo in a bowl with a little of the dressing. Divide between 4 plates, sprinkle with the ciabatta croutons, and top each salad with a poached egg. Drizzle with the remaining dressing, season to taste with salt and pepper, and serve immediately.

For fatoush pita salad, another classic salad that features pieces of bread, in this case pita bread, combine 2 cored, seeded, and diced green bell peppers, ½ diced cucumber, 4 diced ripe tomatoes, 1 finely chopped red onion, 2 crushed garlic cloves, 2 tablespoons chopped parsley, and 1 tablespoon each of chopped mint and cilantro in a large bowl. Toss with the Lemon Dressing on page 78. Toast 2 pita breads in a preheated griddle pan or under a preheated broiler, then tear into bite-size pieces and stir into the salad. Cover and let stand at room temperature for about 30 minutes to allow the flavors to mingle.

greek-style feta salad

Serves **4**
Preparation time **15 minutes**

4 **tomatoes**, cut into wedges
½ **cucumber**, cut into bite-size
 cubes
1 **green bell pepper**, cored,
 seeded, and cut into rings
 or thinly sliced
1 **red onion**, thinly sliced
7 oz **feta cheese**, cubed
½ cup **pitted black olives**
4 tablespoons **olive oil**
2 tablespoons **white wine
 vinegar**
2–3 teaspoons finely chopped
 oregano
salt and pepper

Arrange the tomatoes, cucumber, green pepper, and
red onion in a serving dish.

Top the salad ingredients with the feta and olives.
Season well with salt and pepper and drizzle with the
oil and vinegar. Serve sprinkled with the oregano.

For watermelon, feta, & sunflower seed salad,
add ½ cup cubed watermelon to the salad ingredients
used above. Toast 2 tablespoons sunflower seeds and
sprinkle over the salad before serving.

celery, red onion, & potato salad

Serves **4**
Preparation time **10 minutes**
Cooking time **10–15 minutes**

1 lb **new potatoes**, halved
1 **small fennel bulb**, halved, cored, and finely sliced
2 **celery sticks**, thinly sliced
1 **red onion**, halved and thinly sliced
celery leaves or **dill sprigs**, to garnish (optional)

For the mayonnaise dressing
⅔ cup **mayonnaise**
2 teaspoons **wholegrain mustard**
2 tablespoons finely chopped **dill weed**
salt and pepper

Cook the potatoes in a large saucepan of salted boiling water for 10–15 minutes or until tender.

Meanwhile, combine the fennel, celery, and onion in a large, shallow bowl. To make the dressing, mix all the ingredients together in a small bowl and season to taste with salt and pepper.

Drain the potatoes, rinse under cold running water, then drain again. Add the potatoes to the salad. Add the dressing and toss until well coated. Garnish with celery leaves or dill sprigs, if desired, before serving.

For herbed vinaigrette dressing, as a fresh, fragrant alternative to the mayonnaise dressing above, put 4 tablespoons olive oil, 1 tablespoon chopped parsley, 1 tablespoon chopped basil, 1 teaspoon grated lemon zest, and 1 tablespoon white wine vinegar in a screw-top jar with salt and pepper to taste and shake well. Toss with the vegetables as directed above, and garnish with a few torn basil leaves.

gado gado salad

Serves **4**
Preparation time **15 minutes**
Cooking time **10 minutes**

For the salad
4 **eggs**
1 **iceberg lettuce**, finely
  shredded
2 **carrots**, peeled and cut into
  matchsticks
½ **cucumber**, peeled and cut
  into matchsticks
½ **red bell pepper**, cored,
  seeded, and cut into
  matchsticks

For the peanut dressing
4 tablespoons **crunchy
  peanut butter**
juice of 1 **lime**
1 tablespoon **honey**
1 tablespoon **soy sauce**
½ teaspoon finely chopped
  red chili

Put the eggs in a saucepan of cold water and bring to the boil. Cook for 10 minutes, then plunge into cold water to cool. Shell the eggs, then cut them in half lengthwise.

Combine all the remaining salad ingredients in a bowl, then add the egg halves.

Put all the dressing ingredients in a saucepan and heat gently, stirring, until combined. Drizzle the dressing over the salad and serve immediately or serve the dressing as a dipping sauce for the salad.

For gado gado with noodles & tofu to serve as an impressive main course, cook 10 oz dried fine egg noodles in a saucepan of boiling water for 4 minutes or until just tender while the eggs are cooking as in step 1 above. Drain and refresh the noodles under cold running water. Spread over the base of a shallow serving platter. Pat 4 oz firm tofu dry with paper towels, then cut into bite-size cubes. Heat a shallow depth of peanut oil in a skillet, add the tofu cubes, and cook over a high heat until crisp and browned all over. Remove with a slotted spoon and drain on paper towels. Assemble the salad as above, spoon on top of the noodles, and sprinkle with the tofu. Drizzle over the dressing and serve warm.

soft cooked egg & bacon salad

Serves **4**
Preparation time **10 minutes**
Cooking time **10 minutes**

4 thick slices of **day-old
   bread**
6 tablespoons **olive oil**
4 **eggs**
1 tablespoon **Dijon mustard**
juice of ½ **lemon**
4 oz **bacon**, cut into bite-size
   pieces
2 cups **arugula leaves**
salt and pepper

Cut the bread into small bite-size pieces and toss in
2 tablespoons of the oil. Spread out on a baking sheet
and bake in a preheated oven, 400°F, for 10 minutes
or until golden brown.

Meanwhile, cook the eggs in a saucepan of boiling
water for 4 minutes. Drain, then cool under cold
running water for 1 minute.

Beat together the remaining oil, mustard, and lemon
juice in a small bowl.

Heat a nonstick skillet, add the bacon, and cook over a
medium heat for 5 minutes until crisp and golden. Put
into a bowl with the arugula.

Shell the eggs, then roughly break in half and add to
the bacon and arugula. Sprinkle with the croutons, then
drizzle over the dressing, season to taste with salt and
pepper, and serve immediately.

For creamy yogurt dressing, to drizzle over the
salad instead of the mustard dressing, beat together
4 tablespoons olive oil, the juice of 1 lemon,
6 tablespoons plain yogurt, 1 crushed garlic clove,
1 teaspoon honey, and 1 teaspoon dried oregano.

rice & pasta

tomato & bacon rice

Serves **4**

Preparation time **10 minutes**, plus standing

Cooking time **about 20 minutes**

2 tablespoons **olive oil**

2 **large leeks**, sliced

1 **garlic clove**, crushed

7 oz **Canadian bacon**, chopped

13 oz can **chopped tomatoes**

1¼ cups **long-grain rice**

3 cups **chicken stock**

salt and pepper

chopped **flat-leaf parsley**, to garnish

Heat the oil in a saucepan, add the leeks, garlic, and bacon and cook over a medium heat for a few minutes until soft and starting to brown. Add the tomatoes and rice and cook, stirring, for 1 minute.

Add the stock and season to taste with salt and pepper. Reduce the heat, cover tightly, and cook for 12–15 minutes or until all the stock has been absorbed and the rice is tender.

Remove from the heat and let stand, covered, for 10 minutes. Stir, then garnish with parsley and serve immediately.

For homemade chicken stock, chop a cooked chicken carcass into 3–4 pieces and put in a large saucepan with 1 chopped onion, 2–3 chopped carrots, 1 chopped celery stick, 1 bay leaf, 3–4 parsley stalks, and 1 thyme sprig. Add 7 cups cold water and bring to a boil, skimming any scum that rises to the surface. Reduce the heat and simmer gently for 2–2½ hours. Strain through a cheesecloth-lined sieve. If not using straight away, allow to cool before covering and refrigerating.

mustard & ham macaroni cheese

Serves **4**
Preparation time **5 minutes**
Cooking time **15 minutes**

12 oz **dried quick-cook
    macaroni**
1 cup **mascarpone cheese**
1 cup grated **cheddar cheese**
6 tablespoons **milk**
2 teaspoons **Dijon mustard**
13 oz can **premium cured
    ham**, cut into small cubes
salt and pepper
chopped **flat-leaf parsley**,
    to garnish

Cook the macaroni in a large saucepan of salted boiling water according to the package instructions until al dente, then drain and put in a warmed serving bowl. Cover and keep warm.

Gently heat the mascarpone, cheddar, milk, and mustard in a saucepan until melted into a sauce. Stir in the ham and cook gently for 1–2 minutes. Season to taste with salt and pepper.

Serve the macaroni with the cheese sauce spooned over, garnished with chopped parsley.

For spinach with olive oil & lemon dressing, an ideal accompaniment to the above dish, rinse 1¼ lb spinach leaves in cold water, then put in a large saucepan with just the water that is clinging to the leaves, sprinkling with salt to taste. Cover and cook over a medium heat for 5–7 minutes until wilted and tender, shaking the pan vigorously from time to time. Drain thoroughly in a colander, then return to the rinsed-out pan and toss over a high heat until any remaining water has evaporated. Add 2 tablespoons butter and 2 finely chopped garlic cloves, and continue tossing until combined with the spinach. Transfer to a warmed serving dish, drizzle over 4 tablespoons olive oil and 2 tablespoons lemon juice, season to taste with salt and pepper, and serve immediately with the macaroni dish.

pasta with eggplants & pine nuts

Serves **4**

Preparation time **10 minutes**

Cooking time **15 minutes**

8 tablespoons **olive oil**

2 **eggplants**, diced

2 **red onions**, sliced

½ cup **pine nuts**

3 **garlic cloves**, crushed

5 tablespoons **sundried tomato paste**

⅔ cup **vegetable stock**

10 oz **cracked pepper-, tomato- or mushroom-flavored fresh ribbon pasta**

½ cup **pitted black olives**

salt and pepper

3 tablespoons roughly chopped **flat-leaf parsley**, to garnish

Heat the oil in a large skillet, add the eggplants and onions and cook for 8–10 minutes until tender and golden. Add the pine nuts and garlic and cook, stirring, for 2 minutes. Stir in the sundried tomato paste and stock and simmer for 2 minutes.

Meanwhile, cook the pasta in a large saucepan of salted boiling water for 2 minutes or until al dente.

Drain the pasta and return to the pan. Add the vegetable mixture and olives, season to taste with salt and pepper, and toss together over a medium heat for 1 minute until combined. Serve sprinkled with the chopped parsley.

For potato-topped eggplant & tomato casserole,

cook 4 potatoes in a large saucepan of salted boiling water until just tender. Meanwhile, follow the first stage of the recipe above, but omit the pine nuts, and add just 2 tablespoons sundried tomato paste together with 3 large skinned and chopped tomatoes and the stock. Simmer for 5 minutes, then slice the olives and stir into the mixture. Transfer to a shallow ovenproof dish. Drain the potatoes, cut into slices and arrange, overlapping, on top of the vegetable mixture. Sprinkle with 4 tablespoons finely grated Parmesan cheese and bake in a preheated oven, 400°F, for 35–40 minutes until golden brown on top.

creamy blue cheese pasta

Serves **4**
Preparation time **10 minutes**
Cooking time **10 minutes**

12 oz **dried pasta shells**
2 tablespoons **olive oil**
6 **scallions**, thinly sliced
5 oz **dolcelatte cheese**, diced
¾ cup **cream cheese**
salt and pepper
3 tablespoons chopped
   chives, to garnish

Cook the pasta shells in a large saucepan of salted boiling water according to the package instructions until al dente.

Meanwhile, heat the oil in a large skillet, add the scallions, and cook over a medium heat for 2–3 minutes. Add the cheeses and stir while they blend into a smooth sauce.

Drain the pasta shells and transfer to a warmed serving bowl. Stir in the sauce and season to taste with salt and pepper. Sprinkle with the chives and serve immediately.

For cheese & leek phyllo parcels, fry 3 leeks, thinly sliced, until soft and starting to brown, then allow to cool. Mix with the cheeses as above and 3 tablespoons chives. Melt ⅓ cup butter in a saucepan. Put 8 sheets of phyllo pastry on a plate and cover with a damp dish towel. Working with 1 pastry sheet at a time, cut into 3 equal strips and brush well with melted butter. Put a teaspoon of the cheese mixture at one end of each strip. Fold one corner diagonally over to enclose and continue folding to the end of the strip to make a triangular parcel. Brush with melted butter and lay on a baking sheet. Repeat with the remaining cheese mixture and pastry to make about 24 small parcels. Bake in a preheated oven, 425°F, for 8–10 minutes until golden brown. Serve hot.

tuna & corn pilaff

Serves **4**
Preparation time **10 minutes**
Cooking time **15–20 minutes**

2 tablespoons **olive oil**
1 **onion**, chopped
1 **red bell pepper**, cored,
  seeded, and diced
1 **garlic clove**, crushed
1¼ cups **easy-cook
  long-grain rice**
3 cups **chicken stock**
11 oz can **corn**, drained
7 oz can **tuna in spring
  water**, drained
salt and pepper
6 chopped **scallions**,
  to garnish

Heat the oil in a saucepan, add the onion, red pepper, and garlic and cook until soft. Stir in the rice, then add the stock and season to taste with salt and pepper.

Bring to a boil, then reduce the heat and simmer, stirring occasionally, for 10–15 minutes until all the stock has been absorbed and the rice is tender.

Stir in the corn and tuna and cook briefly over a low heat to heat through. Serve immediately garnished with the scallions.

For picnic pilaff cake, put the cooked rice mixture in a 9 inch square nonstick cake pan. In a bowl, beat 4 eggs with 4 tablespoons finely chopped parsley, season well with salt and pepper, and pour over the rice mixture. Bake in a preheated oven, 350°F, for 25–30 minutes or until set. Allow to cool, then remove from the pan and serve cut into thick wedges.

summer vegetable fettuccine

Serves **4**
Preparation time **10 minutes**
Cooking time **15 minutes**

8 oz **asparagus**, trimmed and
   cut into 2 inch lengths
4 oz **sugarsnap peas**
13 oz **dried fettuccine or
   pappardelle**
7 oz **baby zucchini**
5 oz **button mushrooms**
1 tablespoon **olive oil**
1 **small onion**, finely chopped
1 **garlic clove**, finely chopped
4 tablespoons **lemon juice**
2 teaspoons chopped
   tarragon
2 teaspoons chopped **parsley**
4 oz **smoked mozzarella
   cheese**, diced
salt and pepper

Cook the asparagus and sugarsnap peas in a saucepan of boiling water for 3–4 minutes, then drain and refresh under cold running water. Drain well and set aside.

Cook the pasta in a large saucepan of salted boiling water according to the package instructions until al dente.

Meanwhile, halve the zucchini lengthwise and cut the mushrooms in half. Heat the oil in a large skillet, add the onion and garlic, and cook for 2–3 minutes. Add the zucchini and mushrooms and cook, stirring, for 3–4 minutes. Stir in the asparagus and sugarsnap peas and cook for 1–2 minutes before adding the lemon juice and herbs.

Drain the pasta and return to the pan. Add the vegetable mixture and mozzarella and season to taste with salt and pepper. Toss gently to mix and serve.

For cheesy garlic bread to serve with the pasta, cut a baguette into 1 inch thick slices, cutting almost through to the bottom crust but keeping the slices together at the base. In a bowl, beat ½ cup softened butter with 1 crushed garlic clove, 1½ tablespoons finely chopped parsley, and 1¼ cups finely grated Parmesan cheese. Spread the butter on either side of the bread slices and over the top of the loaf. Wrap tightly in foil, place on a baking sheet, and bake in a preheated oven, 375°F, for 15 minutes. Carefully open up the foil and fold back, then bake for an additional 5 minutes. Cut into slices and serve hot.

carrot, pea, & fava bean risotto

Serves **4**
Preparation time **15 minutes**
Cooking time **about
  25 minutes**

4 tablespoons **butter**
2 tablespoons **olive oil**
1 **large onion**, finely chopped
2 **carrots**, finely chopped
2 **garlic cloves**, finely
  chopped
1¾ cups **risotto rice**
¾ cup **white wine**
6 cups **vegetable stock**,
  heated to simmering
1⅓ cups **frozen peas**,
  defrosted
⅔ cup **frozen fava beans**,
  defrosted and peeled
½ cup finely grated **Parmesan
  cheese**
1 handful of **flat-leaf parsley**,
  roughly chopped
salt and pepper

Melt the butter with the oil in a saucepan, add the onion, carrots, and garlic and cook for about 3 minutes until soft. Add the rice and stir until coated with the butter mixture. Add the wine and cook rapidly, stirring, until it has evaporated.

Add the hot stock, a ladleful at a time, and cook, stirring constantly, until each addition has been absorbed before adding the next. Continue until all the stock has been absorbed and the rice is creamy and cooked but still retains a little bite—this will take around 15 minutes.

Add the peas and fava beans and heat through for 3–5 minutes. Remove from the heat and stir in the Parmesan and parsley. Season to taste with salt and pepper and serve immediately.

For Italian-style risotto balls, allow the risotto to cool, then chill overnight in the refrigerator. Form the chilled mixture into walnut-size balls. Beat 2 eggs together in a shallow bowl. Roll the rice balls through the egg, then in 1 cup dried bread crumbs to coat. Fill a deep, heavy saucepan one-third full with vegetable oil and heat to 350–375°F or until a cube of bread browns in 30 seconds. Add the rice balls, in batches, and cook for 2–3 minutes until golden. Remove with a slotted spoon, drain on paper towels, and serve.

red pepper & cheese tortellini

Serves **4**

Preparation time **10 minutes**,
  plus cooling

Cooking time **15 minutes**

2 **red bell peppers**
2 **garlic cloves**, chopped
8 **scallions**, finely sliced
1 lb **fresh cheese-stuffed
  tortellini or any other fresh
  stuffed tortellini of your
  choice**
¾ cup **olive oil**
¼ cup finely grated **Parmesan
  cheese**
salt and pepper

Cut the peppers into large pieces, removing the cores
and seeds. Lay skin-side up under a preheated broiler
and cook until the skin blackens and blisters. Transfer
to a plastic bag, tie the top to enclose and let cool,
then peel away the skin.

Place the peppers and garlic in a food processor
and blend until fairly smooth. Stir in the scallions and
set aside.

Cook the tortellini in a large saucepan of boiling water
according to the package instructions until al dente.
Drain and return to the pan.

Toss the pepper mixture into the pasta and add the oil
and Parmesan. Season to taste with salt and pepper
and serve immediately.

For warm ham & red pepper tortellini salad, broil
and peel the red peppers as above, then thinly slice.
While the tortellini is cooking, thinly slice 1 red onion.
Drain the pasta and toss with 4 oz chopped cooked
ham, 4½ cups arugula leaves, and the onion and red
peppers. Serve immediately.

lemon & chili shrimp linguine

Serves **4**
Preparation time **15 minutes**
Cooking time **about**
   10 minutes

12 oz **dried linguine or**
   spaghetti
1 tablespoon **butter**
1 tablespoon **olive oil**
1 **garlic clove**, finely chopped
2 **scallions**, thinly sliced
2 **red chilies**, seeded and
   thinly sliced
1 lb **frozen large peeled**
   shrimp, defrosted
2 tablespoons **lemon juice**
2 tablespoons finely chopped
   cilantro leaves
salt and pepper

Cook the pasta in a large saucepan of salted boiling water according to the package instructions until al dente. When the pasta is about half cooked, melt the butter with the oil in a large nonstick skillet. Add the garlic, scallions, and chilies and cook, stirring, for 2–3 minutes.

Add the shrimp and cook briefly until heated through. Pour in the lemon juice and stir in the cilantro until well mixed, then remove from the heat and set aside.

Drain the pasta and toss it with the shrimp mixture, either in the skillet (if large enough) or in a large, warmed serving bowl. Season well with salt and pepper and serve immediately.

For lime & chili squid noodles, slit the bodies of 1 lb small squid down one side and lay flat on a board, insides up. Using a sharp knife, score the flesh with a criss-cross pattern. Cut any tentacles into small pieces. Cook 12 oz dried medium egg noodles in a saucepan of boiling water according to the package instructions until just tender. Meanwhile, heat 2 tablespoons peanut oil in a large nonstick skillet or wok, add 2 thinly sliced garlic cloves and a 1 inch piece of fresh ginger root, peeled and chopped, together with the scallions and chilies as above, and stir-fry over a high heat for 2 minutes. Add the squid and stir-fry for 2–3 minutes. Add the juice of 1 lime, 2 tablespoons dark soy sauce, 1 tablespoon Thai fish sauce, and 2 tablespoons finely chopped cilantro leaves, stir briefly, then remove from the heat. Drain the noodles, toss with the squid mixture, and serve immediately.

pasta with tomato & basil sauce

Serves **4**
Preparation time **10 minutes**
Cooking time **10 minutes**

13 oz **dried spaghetti**
5 tablespoons **olive oil**
5 **garlic cloves**, finely
 chopped
6 **vine-ripened tomatoes**,
 seeded and chopped
½ cup **basil leaves**
salt and pepper

Cook the pasta in a large saucepan of salted boiling water according to the package instructions.

Meanwhile, heat the oil in a skillet, add the garlic, and cook over a low heat for 1 minute. As soon as the garlic begins to change color, remove the pan from the heat and add the remaining oil.

Drain the pasta and return to the pan. Add the garlic oil with the chopped tomatoes and basil leaves. Season to taste with salt and pepper and toss well to mix. Serve immediately.

For quick tomato & basil pizza, prepare the garlic oil as above, but use 4 tablespoons oil and 4 garlic cloves. Meanwhile, skin the tomatoes and seed and chop them as above. Pour off half the oil and reserve, add the tomatoes and half the basil to the pan, season well and allow to simmer while you make the dough. Sift 2 cups self-rising flour and 1 teaspoon salt into a large bowl, then gradually add ⅔ cup warm water, mixing well to form a soft dough. Work the dough into a ball with your hands. Knead on a lightly floured surface until smooth and soft. Roll out the dough to a 12 inch round, making the edge slightly thicker than the center, and lay on a warmed baking sheet. Spread the tomato mixture over the dough base, top with 4 oz sliced mozzarella cheese, and drizzle with the remaining garlic oil. Bake in a preheated oven, 475°F, for 15 minutes or until the base is golden. Sprinkle with the remaining basil leaves and serve immediately.

zucchini & herb risotto

Serves **4**
Preparation time **10 minutes**
Cooking time **about**
 20 minutes

4 tablespoons **butter**
2 tablespoons **olive oil**
1 **large onion**, finely chopped
2 **garlic cloves**, finely
 chopped
1¾ cups **risotto rice**
¾ cup **white wine**
6 cups **vegetable stock**,
 heated to simmering
4¼ cups **baby leaf spinach**,
 chopped
½ cup finely diced **zucchini**
½ cup finely grated **Parmesan
 cheese**
1 small handful of **dill weed,
 mint, and chives**, roughly
 chopped
salt and pepper

Melt the butter with the oil in a saucepan, add the onion and garlic, and cook for about 3 minutes until soft. Add the rice and stir until coated with the butter mixture. Add the wine and cook rapidly, stirring, until it has evaporated.

Add the hot stock, a ladleful at a time, and cook, stirring constantly, until each addition has been absorbed before adding the next. Continue until all the stock has been absorbed and the rice is creamy and cooked but still retains a little bite—this will take around 15 minutes.

Stir in the spinach and zucchini and heat through for 3–5 minutes. Remove from the heat and stir in the Parmesan and herbs. Season to taste with salt and pepper and serve immediately.

For zucchini & carrot risotto, cook the onion and garlic in the butter and oil as above, but add 2 finely chopped celery sticks and 3 small diced carrots. Continue with the recipe above until the end of the second stage. Meanwhile, cut 3 zucchini into ½ inch cubes. Add the zucchini to the risotto and heat through for 3–5 minutes. Remove from the heat and stir in 1 tablespoon chopped basil with the Parmesan. Season to taste with salt and pepper and serve immediately.

mixed bean kedgeree

Serves **4**
Preparation time **10 minutes**
Cooking time **15–20 minutes**

2 tablespoons **olive oil**
1 **onion**, chopped
2 tablespoons **mild curry powder**
1 ¼ cups **long-grain rice**
3 cups **vegetable stock**
4 **eggs**
2 x 13 oz cans **mixed beans**, drained and rinsed
⅔ cup **sour cream**
salt and pepper
2 **tomatoes**, finely chopped, to garnish
flat-leaf parsley, to garnish

Heat the oil in a saucepan, add the onion, and cook until soft. Stir in the curry powder and rice. Add the stock and season to taste with salt and pepper. Bring to a boil, then reduce the heat, cover, and simmer, stirring occasionally, for 10–15 minutes until all the stock has been absorbed and the rice is tender.

Meanwhile, put the eggs in a saucepan of cold water and bring to a boil. Cook for 10 minutes, then plunge into cold water to cool. Shell the eggs, then cut them into wedges.

Stir through the beans and sour cream and cook briefly over a low heat to heat through. Serve garnished with the eggs, tomatoes, and parsley.

For chicken & pineapple pilaff, follow the first stage of the recipe above, but stir in 2 teaspoons turmeric with the curry powder and use chicken stock in place of the vegetable stock. Stir 13 oz chopped cooked chicken breast and an 8 oz can pineapple pieces in natural juice, drained, into the rice with the sour cream and cook briefly over a low heat to heat through. Serve garnished with 3 tablespoons chopped cilantro leaves.

pappardelle puttanesca

Serves **4**

Preparation time **10 minutes**

Cooking time **15 minutes**

2 tablespoons **olive oil**

1 **onion**, chopped

2 **red chilies**, seeded and finely chopped

2 **garlic cloves**, crushed

1 tablespoon **capers**

2 x 13 oz cans **chopped tomatoes**

½ cup **pitted black olives**

2 oz can **anchovy fillets in oil**, drained

13 oz **dried pappardelle or fettuccine**

¼ cup finely grated **Parmesan cheese**

salt and pepper

Heat the oil in a saucepan, add the onion, chilies, and garlic and cook until soft. Add the capers, tomatoes, olives, and anchovies, cover tightly, and simmer for 10 minutes. Season to taste with salt and pepper.

Meanwhile, cook the pasta in a large saucepan of salted boiling water according to the package instructions until al dente.

Drain the pasta. Serve immediately topped with the sauce and the Parmesan.

For tuna & olive pasta sauce, cook the onion and garlic as above but with ½ teaspoon dried red pepper flakes instead of the chilies. Then, in place of the anchovies, add a 7 oz can tuna in oil, drained and flaked, to the pan with the capers, tomatoes, and olives. Simmer for 10 minutes, then stir in ¾ cup half-fat sour cream and season to taste with salt and pepper just before serving on top of the drained pasta. Sprinkle with the Parmesan and 1 tablespoon finely chopped parsley.

pasta pie

Serves **4**
Preparation time **10 minutes**
Cooking time **30 minutes**

1 tablespoon **olive oil**
1 lb **leeks**, sliced
2 **garlic cloves**, crushed
4 **eggs**, beaten
⅔ cup **light cream**
1 cup grated **Gruyère cheese**
4 oz **cooked fusilli**
salt and pepper

Heat the oil in a skillet, add the leeks and garlic, and cook until soft.

Mix the leek mixture with all the remaining ingredients, season to taste with salt and pepper, and transfer to a greased ovenproof dish or medium-size cake pan.

Bake in a preheated oven, 350°F, for 25 minutes or until the eggs have set and the pie is golden brown. Serve with a crisp green salad.

For chicken & mozzarella macaroni pie, follow the first stage of the recipe, then add 7 oz cooked chicken, cut into small bite-size pieces, and 2 tablespoons finely chopped tarragon with the eggs and cream, together with 1 cup grated mozzarella cheese and 4 oz cooked macaroni. Bake in the oven as above.

meat & poultry

pea & lamb korma

Serves **4**
Preparation time **10 minutes**
Cooking time **30 minutes**

2 tablespoons **olive oil**
1 **onion**, chopped
2 **garlic cloves**, crushed
8 oz **potatoes**, cut into ¾ inch
  dice
1 lb **ground lamb**
1 tablespoon **korma curry
  powder**
1⅓ cups **frozen peas**
¾ cup **vegetable stock**
2 tablespoons **mango
  chutney**
salt and pepper
chopped **cilantro leaves**,
  to garnish

Heat the oil in a saucepan, add the onion and garlic, and cook for 5 minutes until the onion is soft and starting to brown. Add the potatoes and ground lamb and cook, stirring and breaking up the lamb with a wooden spoon, for 5 minutes or until the meat has browned.

Add the curry powder and cook, stirring, for 1 minute. Add the remaining ingredients and season to taste with salt and pepper. Bring to a boil, then reduce the heat, cover tightly, and simmer for 20 minutes.

Remove from the heat, garnish with chopped cilantro, and serve with plain yogurt and steamed rice.

For spicy Indian wraps, finely shred an iceberg lettuce and place in a bowl with 1 coarsely grated carrot. Heat 8 large flour wraps (or tortillas) on a griddle pan for 1–2 minutes on each side and then add the lettuce mixture onto the center of each one. Divide the korma mixture (cooked as above) between the wraps and roll each one to enclose the filling. Serve accompanied with a dollop of yogurt if desired.

thai green pork curry

Serves **4**
Preparation time **10 minutes**
Cooking time **20 minutes**

2 tablespoons **olive oil**
4 **boneless pork steaks**, cut
  into bite-size pieces
2 tablespoons **Thai green
  curry paste** (see page 196)
1¾ cups **coconut milk**
4 oz **green beans**
7 oz can **water chestnuts**,
  drained, rinsed, and cut in
  half
juice of **1 lime**, or to taste
1 handful of **cilantro leaves**

Heat the oil in a large saucepan, add the pork, and cook, stirring, for 3–4 minutes until browned all over. Add the curry paste and cook, stirring, for 1 minute until fragrant.

Add the coconut milk, stir, and reduce the heat to a gentle simmer. Cook for 10 minutes, then add the beans and water chestnuts. Cook for an additional 3 minutes.

Remove from the heat, add lime juice to taste, and stir through the cilantro. Serve immediately with boiled rice.

For Thai red pork curry, replace the Thai green curry paste with Thai red curry paste. To prepare your own Thai red curry paste, put 10 large red chilies, 2 teaspoons coriander seeds, 2 inch piece of fresh ginger root, peeled and finely chopped, 1 finely chopped lemon grass stalk, 4 halved garlic cloves, 1 roughly chopped shallot, 1 teaspoon lime juice, and 2 tablespoons peanut oil in a food processor or blender and process to a thick paste. Alternatively, pound the ingredients together using a mortar and pestle. Transfer the paste to an airtight container; it can be stored in the refrigerator for up to 3 weeks.

chicken ratatouille

Serves **2**
Preparation time **15 minutes**
Cooking time **25 minutes**

2 tablespoons **olive oil**
2 **boneless, skinless chicken breasts**, cut into bite-size pieces
½ medium **zucchini**, thinly sliced
½ cup cubed **aubergine**
1 **onion**, thinly sliced
½ cup cored, seeded **green bell pepper**, thinly sliced
⅓ cup sliced **mushrooms**
13 oz can **plum tomatoes**
2 **garlic cloves**, finely chopped
1 teaspoon **organic vegetable bouillon powder**
1 teaspoon **dried basil**
1 teaspoon **dried parsley**
½ teaspoon **ground black pepper**

Heat the oil in a large skillet, add the chicken, and cook, stirring, for 3–4 minutes until browned all over. Add the zucchini, eggplant, onion, green pepper, and mushrooms and cook, stirring occasionally, for 15 minutes or until tender.

Add the tomatoes to the pan and gently stir. Stir in the garlic, bouillon powder, herbs, and pepper and simmer, uncovered, for 5 minutes or until the chicken is tender. Serve immediately.

For roasted potatoes with rosemary and garlic, to serve as an accompaniment, heat 2 tablespoons olive oil in a large roasting pan in a preheated oven, 450°F. Meanwhile, cut 1½ lb scrubbed, unpeeled potatoes into quarters lengthwise and pat dry with paper towels. Mix together 2 tablespoons olive oil and 2 tablespoons chopped rosemary in a bowl, add the potatoes, and toss to coat. Add to the roasting pan, shake carefully to form an even layer, then roast at the top of the oven for 20 minutes. Meanwhile, peel and thinly slice 4 garlic cloves. Remove the pan and move the potatoes around so that they cook evenly. Sprinkle the garlic slices among the potatoes, then return to the oven and cook for an additional 5 minutes. Season to taste with salt and pepper and serve immediately with the chicken ratatouille.

moroccan meatball tagine

Serves **4**
Preparation time **15 minutes**
Cooking time **40 minutes**

2 small **onions**, finely chopped
2 tablespoons **raisins**
1½ lb **ground beef**
1 tablespoon **tomato paste**
3 teaspoons **curry powder**
3 tablespoons **olive oil**
½ teaspoon **ground cinnamon**
1¼ lb can **chopped tomatoes**
juice of ½ **lemon**
2 **celery sticks**, thickly sliced
1 large or 2 medium **zucchini**,
　roughly chopped
1 cup **frozen peas**

Mix together half the onions, the raisins, ground beef, tomato paste, and curry powder in a bowl. Using your hands, knead to combine the mixture evenly. Form the mixture into 24 meatballs.

Heat 1 tablespoon of the oil in a saucepan, add the meatballs, in small batches, and cook until browned all over. Tip out the excess fat and put all the meatballs in the pan. Add the cinnamon, tomatoes, and lemon juice, cover, and simmer gently for 25 minutes until the meatballs are cooked.

Meanwhile, heat the remaining oil in a large skillet, add the celery and zucchini, and cook until soft and an additional further 5 minutes until the peas are tender.

Just before serving, stir the zucchini mixture into the meatball mixture.

For cilantro & apricot couscous, to serve as an accompaniment, put 1 cup instant couscous in a large, heatproof bowl with ⅓ cup ready-to-eat dried apricots, chopped. Pour over boiling hot vegetable stock to just cover the couscous. Cover and let stand for 10–12 minutes until all the water has been absorbed. Meanwhile, chop 2 large, ripe tomatoes and finely chop 2 tablespoons cilantro leaves. Fluff up the couscous grains with a fork and tip into a warmed serving dish. Stir in the tomatoes and cilantro with 2 tablespoons olive oil and season to taste with salt and pepper. Toss well to mix and serve with the tagine.

spicy pork rolls with minted yogurt

Serves **4**
Preparation time **15 minutes**
Cooking time **10–12 minutes**

4 **pork scallops**, about
    4–5 oz each
1 **small onion**, roughly
    chopped
1 **red chili**, seeded and
    roughly chopped
4 tablespoons roughly
    chopped **cilantro leaves**
grated zest and juice of **1 lime**
1 tablespoon **Thai fish sauce**
2 **garlic cloves**, crushed
1 teaspoon grated **fresh
    ginger root**
1 teaspoon **ground cumin**
½ teaspoon **ground coriander**
3 tablespoons **coconut milk**
mint leaves, to garnish
    (optional)

For the minted yogurt
¾ cup **Greek** or **whole milk
    yogurt**
4 tablespoons roughly
    chopped **mint leaves**
salt and pepper

Lay a pork scallop between 2 sheets of plastic wrap and pound lightly with a mallet until about ¼ inch thick. Repeat with the remaining scallops.

Process the remaining ingredients in a food processor or blender to a coarse paste. Spread a quarter of the paste over a pork scallop and roll up to enclose the filling. Secure the roll with a wooden toothpick. Repeat with the remaining paste and pork.

Put the rolls on a baking sheet and cook in a preheated oven, 400°F, for 10–12 minutes or until cooked through.

Meanwhile, to make the minted yogurt, put the yogurt in a small bowl, stir in the mint, and season to taste with salt and pepper. Serve the rolls hot, with a dollop of the minted yogurt on the side and garnished with mint leaves, if desired.

For satay sauce to serve with the pork rolls instead of the minted yogurt, heat 1 tablespoon peanut oil in a small skillet, add 1 crushed garlic clove and cook, stirring, over a low heat for 2–3 minutes until softened. Stir in 4 tablespoons crunchy peanut butter, ¼ teaspoon dried red pepper flakes, 1 tablespoon dark soy sauce, 1 tablespoon lime juice, 1 teaspoon honey, and 2 tablespoons coconut cream and heat gently, stirring, until boiling. Serve warm with the pork rolls.

fast chicken curry

Serves **4**
Preparation time **5 minutes**
Cooking time **20–25 minutes**

3 tablespoons **olive oil**
1 **onion**, finely chopped
4 tablespoons **medium curry paste**
8 **chicken thighs**, boned, skinned, and cut into thin strips
13 oz can **chopped tomatoes**
8 oz **broccoli**, broken into small florets, and stalks peeled and sliced
6 tablespoons **coconut milk**
salt and pepper

Heat the oil in a deep nonstick saucepan, add the onion, and cook for 3 minutes until soft. Add the curry paste and cook, stirring, for 1 minute.

Add the chicken, tomatoes, broccoli, and coconut milk to the pan. Bring to a boil, then reduce the heat, cover, and cook over a low heat for 15–20 minutes.

Remove from the heat, season well with salt and pepper, and serve immediately.

For seafood patties with curry sauce, follow the first stage of the recipe above, then add the tomatoes, 4 cups young spinach leaves, and the coconut milk and cook as directed. Meanwhile, put 12 oz roughly chopped white fish fillets and 6 oz frozen cooked peeled shrimp, defrosted and roughly chopped, in a food processor and process until well combined. Alternatively, finely chop and mix together by hand. Transfer to a bowl, add 4 finely chopped scallions, 2 tablespoons chopped cilantro leaves, 1 cup fresh white bread crumbs, a squeeze of lemon juice, 1 beaten egg, and salt and pepper to taste. Mix well, then form into 16 patties. Roll in ½ cup fresh white bread crumbs to coat. Heat a shallow depth of vegetable oil in a large skillet, add the patties, in batches, and cook for 5 minutes on each side or until crisp and golden brown. Serve hot with the curry sauce.

chicken thighs with fresh pesto

Serves **4**
Preparation time **15 minutes**
Cooking time **25 minutes**

1 tablespoon **olive oil**
8 **chicken thighs**
chopped basil leaves,
  to garnish

For the pesto
6 tablespoons **olive oil**
⅓ cup **pine nuts**, toasted
½ cup freshly grated
  Parmesan cheese
1¼ cups **basil leaves**
2 tablespoons **parsley**
2 **garlic cloves**, chopped
salt and pepper

Heat the oil in a nonstick skillet over a medium heat. Add the chicken thighs and cook gently, turning frequently until the chicken is cooked through (about 20 minutes).

Meanwhile, make the pesto by placing all the ingredients in a food processor or blender and whizzing until smooth and well combined.

Remove the chicken from the pan and keep hot. Reduce the heat and add the pesto to the pan. Heat through for 2–3 minutes.

Pour the warmed pesto over the chicken thighs, garnish with basil, and serve with zucchini ribbons and broiled tomatoes.

For tomato rice as an accompaniment, cut 13 oz cherry tomatoes in half and place on a nonstick baking sheet. Sprinkle with 2 tablespoons of finely chopped garlic and sea salt and pepper to taste. Place in a hot oven for 12–15 minutes, then transfer to a mixing bowl with 1½ cups cooked basmati or long-grain rice. Toss well to mix and serve with the chicken cooked as above.

bobotie

Serves **4**

Preparation time **10 minutes**, plus cooling

Cooking time **40 minutes**

2 tablespoons **olive oil**

1 **onion**, chopped

2 **garlic cloves**, chopped

2 tablespoons **medium curry paste**

1 lb **ground beef**

2 tablespoons **tomato paste**

1 tablespoon **white wine vinegar**

⅓ cup **golden raisins**

1 slice of **white bread**, soaked in 3 tablespoons milk and mashed

4 **eggs**, beaten

6 tablespoons **heavy cream**

salt and pepper

Heat the oil in a saucepan, add the onion and garlic and cook until soft and starting to brown. Add the curry paste and ground beef and cook, stirring and breaking up with a wooden spoon, for 5 minutes or until browned.

Add the tomato paste, vinegar, golden raisins, and mashed bread. Season to taste with salt and pepper and transfer to a deep, medium ovenproof dish or an 8 inch heavy cake pan.

Mix together the eggs and cream in a bowl, season to taste with salt and pepper, and pour over the meat mixture.

Bake in a preheated oven, 350°F, for 30 minutes or until the egg is set and golden brown. Remove from the oven and allow to cool for 10–15 minutes before serving.

For individual boboties to serve as a stylish appetizer for an elegant dinner, divide the meat mixture between 4 individual ramekin dishes and pour the egg mixture over each one. Bake in a preheated oven, 350°F, for 20–25 minutes or until the tops are just set. Meanwhile, toast thin slices of bread in a preheated griddle pan or under a preheated broiler. Serve with the boboties.

pesto turkey kebabs

Serves **4**

Preparation time **15 minutes**

Cooking time **about 12 minutes**

4 **turkey breast steaks**, about 1 lb in total

2 tablespoons **pesto**

4 slices of **prosciutto**

2 cups **sundried tomatoes**, finely chopped

4 oz **mozzarella cheese**, finely diced

1 tablespoon **olive oil**

salt and pepper

chopped parsley, to garnish

lemon wedges, to serve

Lay a turkey steak between 2 sheets of plastic wrap and pound lightly with a mallet until about ½ inch thick. Repeat with the remaining steaks.

Spread the pesto over each beaten turkey steak and lay 1 slice of prosciutto on top of each. Sprinkle the tomatoes and mozzarella evenly over the turkey steaks, then season to taste with salt and pepper and roll up each one from the long side.

Cut the turkey rolls into 1 inch slices. Carefully thread the slices of roll evenly onto 4 metal skewers.

Brush the turkey rolls lightly with the oil and broil under a preheated broiler for 6 minutes on each side or until cooked through. Increase or reduce the temperature setting of the broiler, if necessary, to ensure that the rolls cook through and brown on the outside. Garnish with chopped parsley and serve hot with lemon wedges for squeezing over.

For homemade pesto, put ⅓ cup pine nuts and 2 crushed garlic cloves in a food processor or blender and process to a thick paste. Alternatively, put in a mortar and pound with a pestle. Tear 1¼ cups basil leaves into shreds and process or pound to a thick paste. Transfer both pastes to a bowl. Stir in 1½ cups finely grated Parmesan cheese and 2 tablespoons lemon juice. Add ⅔ cup olive oil a little at a time, beating well. Season to taste with salt and pepper.

coconut chicken

Serves **4**
Preparation time **10 minutes**
Cooking time **20 minutes**

1 tablespoon **vegetable oil**
1 **onion**, diced
1 **red bell pepper**, cored,
 seeded, and diced
8 **chicken thighs**, boned,
 skinned, and cut into
 bite-size pieces
7 oz **snow peas**
2 tablespoons **medium
 curry paste**
1 teaspoon finely chopped
 lemon grass stalks
1 teaspoon finely chopped
 fresh ginger root
2 **garlic cloves**, crushed
1 tablespoon **soy sauce**
1¾ cups **coconut milk**
1 handful of **basil leaves**
salt and pepper (optional)

Heat the oil in a saucepan, add the onion and red pepper, and cook for 5 minutes until soft and just starting to brown. Add the chicken and cook for 5 minutes until browned all over.

Add the snow peas, curry paste, lemon grass, ginger, garlic, and soy sauce and cook, stirring, for 2–3 minutes. Add the coconut milk and stir well. Cover and simmer gently for 5–8 minutes.

Remove from the heat, check and adjust the seasoning if necessary, and stir in the basil just before serving with boiled basmati rice.

For spicy fried rice to serve as an alternative accompaniment, heat 2 tablespoons vegetable oil in a wok or large skillet and crack 2 eggs into it, breaking the yolks and stirring them around. Add 2 cups cold, cooked long-grain rice, 3 teaspoons superfine sugar, 1½ tablespoons soy sauce, 2 teaspoons dried red pepper flakes, and 1 teaspoon Thai fish sauce, and stir-fry over a high heat for 2 minutes. Serve immediately with the coconut chicken, garnished with cilantro leaves.

duck breasts with fruity salsa

Serves **4**
Preparation time **15 minutes**
Cooking time **about
15 minutes**

2 large **boneless duck
breasts**, skin on, halved
lengthwise
2 tablespoons **dark soy
sauce**
1 tablespoon **honey**
1 teaspoon grated **fresh
ginger root**
1 teaspoon **chili powder**

For the fruity salsa
1 large ripe **mango**, peeled,
pitted, and finely diced
6–8 **plums**, pitted and
finely diced
grated zest and juice of **1 lime**
1 small **red onion**, finely
chopped
1 tablespoon **olive oil**
1 tablespoon roughly chopped
mint leaves
1 tablespoon roughly chopped
cilantro leaves
salt and pepper

Use a sharp knife to score the skin on the duck
breasts lightly, cutting down into the fat but not through
to the meat.

Heat a skillet until very hot, then add the duck breasts,
skin-side down, and cook for 3 minutes or until sealed
and browned. Turn over and cook for 2 minutes. Use a
slotted spoon to transfer the duck breasts to a baking
sheet, skin-side up.

In a small bowl, mix together the soy sauce, honey,
ginger, and chili powder. Spoon over the duck. Cook in
a preheated oven, 400°F, for 6–9 minutes, until cooked
to your liking. The duck may be served pink in the
center or more well cooked.

Meanwhile, in a bowl, mix together all the ingredients
for the salsa and season well with salt and pepper.

Thinly slice the cooked duck and fan out the slices
slightly on individual plates. Spoon some of the salsa
over the duck and serve immediately, offering the
remaining salsa separately.

For apricot & lime salsa as an alternative to the plum
and mango salsa, in a bowl mix together 1 cup canned
apricots in natural juice, drained and finely chopped,
the grated zest and juice of 1 lime, 1 finely chopped
shallot, 1 tablespoon finely chopped fresh ginger root,
1 tablespoon olive oil, and 2 teaspoons honey.

rice noodles with lemon chicken

Serves **4**
Preparation time **10 minutes**
Cooking time **10 minutes**

4 **boneless chicken breasts**,
  skin on
juice of 2 **lemons**
4 tablespoons **sweet
  chili sauce**
8 oz **dried rice noodles**
1 small bunch of **flat-leaf
  parsley**, chopped
1 small bunch of **cilantro**,
  chopped
½ **cucumber**, peeled into
  ribbons with a vegetable
  peeler
salt and pepper
finely chopped **red chili**,
  to garnish

Mix the chicken with half the lemon juice and the sweet chili sauce in a large bowl and season to taste with salt and pepper.

Lay a chicken breast between 2 sheets of plastic wrap and lightly pound with a mallet to flatten. Repeat with the remaining chicken breasts.

Arrange the chicken on a broiler rack in a single layer. Cook under a preheated broiler for 4–5 minutes on each side or until cooked through. Finish on the skin side so that it is crisp.

Meanwhile, put the noodles in a heatproof bowl, pour over boiling water to cover, and leave for 10 minutes until just tender, then drain. Add the remaining lemon juice, herbs, and cucumber to the noodles and toss well to mix. Season to taste with salt and pepper.

Top the noodles with the cooked chicken and serve immediately, garnished with the chopped red chili.

For stir-fried ginger broccoli to serve as an accompaniment, trim the stalks from 1 lb broccoli. Divide the heads into florets, then diagonally slice the stalks. Blanch the florets and stalks in a saucepan of salted boiling water for 30 seconds. Drain, refresh under cold running water, and drain again thoroughly. Heat 2 tablespoons vegetable oil in a large skillet, add 1 thinly sliced garlic clove and a 1 inch piece of fresh ginger root, peeled and finely chopped, and stir-fry for a few seconds. Add the broccoli and stir-fry over a high heat for 2 minutes. Sprinkle with 1 teaspoon sesame oil and stir-fry for 30 seconds more.

quick sausage & bean casserole

Serves **4**
Preparation time **5 minutes**
Cooking time **25 minutes**

2 tablespoons **olive oil**
16 **mini sausages**
2 **garlic cloves**, crushed
13 oz can **chopped tomatoes**
13 oz can **baked beans**
7 oz can **mixed beans**,
   drained and rinsed
½ teaspoon **dried thyme**
salt and pepper
3 tablespoons chopped **flat-
   leaf parsley**, to garnish

Heat the oil in a skillet, add the sausages, and cook until browned all over.

Transfer the sausages to a large saucepan and add all the remaining ingredients. Bring to a boil, then reduce the heat, cover tightly, and simmer for 20 minutes. Season to taste with salt and pepper and serve hot, garnished with the chopped herbs.

For mustard mash to serve as an accompaniment, cook 2 lb chopped potatoes in a large saucepan of salted boiling water until tender. Drain well and return to the pan. Mash with ⅓ cup butter, 1 tablespoon wholegrain mustard, 3 teaspoons prepared English mustard, and 1 crushed garlic clove. Season to taste with salt and pepper, then beat in 2 tablespoons chopped parsley and a dash of olive oil. Serve hot with the casserole.

jerk chicken wings

Serves **4**
Preparation time **5 minutes**,
  plus marinating
Cooking time **12 minutes**

12 large **chicken wings**
2 tablespoons **olive oil**
1 tablespoon **jerk**
  seasoning mix
juice of ½ **lemon**
1 teaspoon **salt**
chopped **flat-leaf parsley**,
  to garnish
lemon wedges, to serve

Put the chicken wings in a glass or ceramic dish. In a small bowl, beat together the oil, jerk seasoning mix, lemon juice, and salt, pour over the wings and stir well until evenly coated. Cover and allow to marinate in the refrigerator for at least 30 minutes or overnight.

Arrange the chicken wings on a broiler rack and cook under a preheated broiler, basting halfway through cooking with any remaining marinade, for 6 minutes on each side or until cooked through, tender, and lightly charred at the edges. Increase or reduce the temperature setting of the broiler, if necessary, to ensure that the wings cook through. Garnish with the chopped parsley and serve immediately with lemon wedges for squeezing over.

For jerk lamb kebabs, coat 1½ lb boneless lamb, cut into bite-size pieces in the jerk marinade as above, marinating overnight if time allows. Thread the meat onto 8 metal skewers and cook under a preheated broiler or over a barbecue for 6–8 minutes on each side or until cooked to your desire.

pork & red pepper chili

Serves **4**
Preparation time **10 minutes**
Cooking time **30 minutes**

2 tablespoons **olive oil**
1 large **onion**, chopped
2 **garlic cloves**, crushed
1 **red bell pepper**, cored, seeded, and diced
1 lb **ground pork**
1 **red chili**, finely chopped
1 teaspoon **dried oregano**
2 cups **passata (sieved tomatoes)**
13 oz can **red kidney beans**, drained and rinsed
salt and pepper
sour cream, to serve

Heat the oil in a saucepan, add the onion, garlic, and red pepper, and cook for 5 minutes until soft and starting to brown. Add the ground pork and cook, stirring and breaking up with a wooden spoon, for 5 minutes or until browned.

Add all the remaining ingredients and bring to a boil. Reduce the heat and simmer gently for 20 minutes. Remove from the heat, season well with salt and pepper, and serve immediately with a dollop of sour cream and boiled rice or crusty bread.

For lamb & eggplant chili, substitute the ground pork and red pepper with 1 medium eggplant and 1 lb ground lamb. Cut the eggplant into small cubes and fry as above with the lamb. Garnish the finished dish with 2 tablespoons of finely chopped mint leaves and serve with rice or pasta.

teriyaki chicken

Serves **4**
Preparation time **10 minutes**,
    plus marinating
Cooking time **8 minutes**

2 **boneless, skinless chicken
    breasts**, cut into thin strips
2 tablespoons **soy sauce**
1 tablespoon **olive oil**
2 **large carrots**, peeled and
    cut into small matchsticks
2 **red bell peppers**, cored,
    seeded, and cut into small
    matchsticks
7 oz jar **teriyaki stir-fry sauce**
6 **scallions**, chopped

Put the chicken in a glass or ceramic bowl, add the soy sauce, and toss well to coat. Cover and let marinate in a cool place for 10 minutes.

Heat the oil in a wok or large skillet, add the chicken and marinade and stir-fry for 2 minutes. Add the carrots and peppers and stir-fry for 4 minutes. Add the sauce and scallions and cook briefly, stirring, to heat through. Serve immediately over egg noodles.

For pork teriyaki with crispy garlic, substitute the chicken with 1¼ lb pork steaks. Place the steaks between sheets of plastic wrap and flatten with a wooden mallet. Cut into thin strips and cook as above. To make the crispy garlic, thinly slice 4 garlic cloves. Heat a 2 inch depth of oil in a deep, heavy saucepan to 350–375°F or until a cube of bread browns in 30 seconds. Add the garlic slices and cook until golden and crispy. Remove with a slotted spoon and drain on paper towels. Sprinkle over the finished dish.

beef with black bean sauce

Serves **4**

Preparation time **15 minutes**

Cooking time **15 minutes**

1½ lb **minute steak**

2 tablespoons **peanut oil**

1 **onion**, thinly sliced

4 oz **snow peas**, halved
lengthwise

1 **garlic clove**, finely chopped

½ inch piece **fresh ginger
root**, peeled and finely
chopped

1 small **red chili**, finely
chopped

7 oz jar **black bean sauce**

salt and pepper

Trim the steak of all fat and then cut the meat into thin slices across the grain. Heat half the oil in a wok or large skillet, add the beef, in 2 batches, and cook, stirring, until well browned all over. Transfer to a bowl.

Heat the remaining oil in the pan, add the onion and snow peas, and stir-fry for 2 minutes. Add the garlic, ginger, and chili and stir-fry for 1 minute. Add the black bean sauce and cook, stirring, for 5 minutes or until the sauce begins to thicken. Season to taste with salt and pepper and serve immediately with steamed rice or egg-fried rice.

For seafood with black bean sauce, stir-fry 1 lb raw jumbo shrimp and 7 oz squid rings in a hot wok for 2–3 minutes. Add 8 sliced scallions and 2 sliced red bell peppers and stir-fry for an additional 2–3 minutes. Add the black bean sauce and cook for 5 minutes, stirring often. Serve hot with egg noodles.

tandoori chicken

Serves **4**
Preparation time **5 minutes**,
  plus marinating
Cooking time **25–30 minutes**

8 **chicken drumsticks**
8 **chicken thighs**
2 tablespoons **tikka spice
  mix or paste**
2 **garlic cloves**, crushed
1 tablespoon **tomato paste**
juice of 1 **lemon**
5 tablespoons **plain yogurt**

To garnish
grated lime zest
chopped cilantro

Make deep slashes all over the chicken pieces. In
a large glass or ceramic bowl, mix together all the
remaining ingredients, then add the chicken and turn
to coat thoroughly with the marinade. Cover and allow
to marinate in the refrigerator for at least 30 minutes
or overnight.

Transfer the chicken to an ovenproof dish and cook in a
preheated oven, 475°F, for 25–30 minutes until cooked
through, tender, and lightly charred at the edges. Serve
garnished with lime zest and chopped cilantro.

For blackened tandoori salmon, use the marinade
above to coat 4 thick, skinless salmon fillets, then
cover and allow to marinate in the refrigerator for
30 minutes–1 hour. Transfer to a nonstick baking
sheet and bake at 350°F, for 20 minutes or until
cooked through. Serve with plain rice or couscous.

griddled salsa chicken

Serves **4**
Preparation time **10 minutes**
Cooking time **6 minutes**

4 boneless chicken breasts,
 skin on
3 tablespoons **olive oil**
salt and pepper

**For the cucumber and
tomato salsa**
1 **red onion**, finely chopped
2 **tomatoes**, seeded
 and diced
1 **cucumber**, finely diced
1 **red chili**, finely chopped
1 small handful of **cilantro
 leaves**, chopped
juice of **1 lime**

Remove the skin from the chicken breasts. Using kitchen scissors, cut each breast in half lengthwise but without cutting the whole way through. Open each breast out flat. Brush with the oil and season well with salt and pepper. Heat a griddle pan until very hot. Add the chicken breasts and cook for 3 minutes on each side or until cooked through and grill-marked.

Meanwhile, to make the salsa, mix together the onion, tomatoes, cucumber, red chili, cilantro, and lime juice. Season well with salt and pepper.

Serve the chicken hot with the spicy salsa spooned over and around.

For griddled tuna with pineapple salsa, prepare and cook 4 thick fresh tuna steaks, about 6 oz each, as for the butterflied chicken breasts above. Meanwhile, in a bowl, mix together 6 tablespoons drained and roughly diced canned pineapple, 1 finely chopped red onion, 1 tablespoon finely chopped fresh ginger root, 1 finely chopped red chili, grated zest and juice of 1 lime, 2 teaspoons honey, and salt and pepper to taste. Serve the pineapple salsa with the griddled tuna.

chicken with spring herbs

Serves **4**
Preparation time **15 minutes**
Cooking time **20 minutes**

1 cup **mascarpone cheese**
1 handful of **chervil**, finely
  chopped
½ bunch of **parsley**, finely
  chopped
2 tablespoons chopped
  mint leaves
4 **boneless chicken breasts**,
  skin on
¾ cup **white wine**
2 tablespoons **butter**
salt and pepper

Mix together the mascarpone and herbs in a bowl and season well with salt and pepper.

Lift the skin away from each chicken breast and spread a quarter of the mascarpone mixture on each breast. Replace the skin and smooth carefully over the mascarpone mixture. Season to taste with salt and pepper.

Place the chicken in a baking dish and pour the wine around it. Dot the butter over the chicken.

Roast in a preheated oven, 350°F, for 20 minutes until the chicken is golden and crisp. Remove from the oven and serve with garlic bread.

For baby glazed carrots as an alternative accompaniment to garlic bread, melt 2 tablespoons butter in a saucepan, add 1 lb young carrots, quartered lengthwise, a pinch of sugar, and salt and pepper to taste. Pour over just enough water to cover and simmer gently for 15–20 minutes until the carrots are tender and the liquid has evaporated, adding 2 tablespoons orange juice toward the end of the cooking time. Serve with the chicken garnished with chopped parsley.

mexican pie

Serves **4**
Preparation time **10 minutes**
Cooking time **30 minutes**

2 tablespoons **olive oil**
1 **onion**, finely chopped
2 **garlic cloves**, crushed
2 **carrots**, diced
8 oz **ground beef**
1 **red chili**, finely chopped
13 oz can **chopped tomatoes**
13 oz can **red kidney beans**,
   drained and rinsed
2 oz **tortilla chips**
1 cup grated **cheddar cheese**
salt and pepper
chopped parsley or cilantro,
   to garnish

Heat the oil in a saucepan, add the onion, garlic, and carrots, and cook until softened. Add the ground beef and chili and cook, stirring and breaking up with a wooden spoon, for 5 minutes or until the meat has browned. Add the tomatoes and beans, mix well, and season to taste with salt and pepper.

Transfer to an ovenproof dish, cover with the tortilla chips, and sprinkle with the cheddar. Bake in a preheated oven, 400°F, for 20 minutes or until golden brown. Garnish with chopped parsley or cilantro before serving.

For tortilla-wrapped chili with guacamole, follow the first stage of the recipe above, but then cover and simmer on the stove for 20 minutes. Meanwhile, halve 2 large, ripe avocados lengthwise and remove the pits. Scoop the flesh into a bowl, add 3 tablespoons lime juice, and roughly mash. Add 4 oz tomatoes, skinned, seeded, and chopped, 2 crushed garlic cloves, ½ cup chopped scallions, 1 tablespoon finely chopped green chilies, and 2 tablespoons chopped cilantro leaves, mix well, and season to taste with salt and pepper. Divide the chili between 4 warmed flour tortillas and wrap up. Serve with the guacamole, and sour cream, if desired.

minted lamb skewers

Serves **4**
Preparation time **10 minutes**
Cooking time **10 minutes**

1 lb **ground lamb**
2 teaspoons **curry powder**
6 tablespoons finely chopped
  mint leaves
salt and pepper

Mix together the ground lamb, curry powder, and mint in a bowl and season to taste with salt and pepper. Using your hands, knead to combine the mixture evenly.

Divide the mixture into small sausages and thread evenly onto metal skewers. Cook under a preheated broiler for 10 minutes, turning once. Serve hot with warmed naan bread, sour cream, and a lime wedge. Sprinkle with chopped mint leaves and a little curry powder.

For cucumber raita to serve as an accompaniment, cut ½ large cucumber in half lengthwise, scoop out and discard the seeds, then thinly slice each half. In a bowl, mix together with 1 cup plain yogurt, 1 tablespoon chopped mint leaves, and 1 tablespoon chopped cilantro leaves. Season to taste with salt and pepper. Toast 2 teaspoons cumin seeds in a dry skillet until fragrant. Sprinkle over the raita just before serving.

fish & shellfish

creamy garlic mussels

Serves **4**
Preparation time **15 minutes**
Cooking time **about
  8 minutes**

3 lb **fresh, live mussels**
1 tablespoon **butter**
1 **onion**, finely chopped
6 **garlic cloves**, finely
  chopped
6 tablespoons **white wine**
⅔ cup **light cream**
1 large handful of **flat-leaf
  parsley**, roughly chopped
salt and pepper

Scrub the mussels in cold water, scrape off any barnacles, and pull away the dark hairy beards that protrude from the shells. Discard any with broken shells or any open mussels that do not close when tapped sharply.

Melt the butter in a large saucepan, add the onion and garlic, and cook for 2–3 minutes until transparent and softened.

Increase the heat and tip in the mussels with the wine, then cover and cook for 3 minutes or until all the shells have opened. Discard any that remain closed.

Pour in the cream and heat through briefly, stirring well. Add the parsley, season well with salt and pepper, and serve immediately in large bowls, with crusty bread to mop up the juices.

For mussels in spicy tomato sauce, cook the onion and garlic in 1 tablespoon olive oil instead of the butter, together with 1 seeded and finely chopped red chili. Add 1 teaspoon paprika and cook, stirring, for 1 minute, then add 13 oz can chopped tomatoes. Season to taste with salt and pepper, cover, and simmer gently for 15 minutes. Meanwhile, clean the mussels, as in the first stage above. Stir the mussels into the tomato sauce and increase the heat. Cover and cook for 3 minutes or until all the shells have opened. Discard any that remain closed. Add the parsley and serve as above.

sesame shrimp with bok choy

Serves **4**

Preparation time **10 minutes**, plus marinating

Cooking time **about 3 minutes**

1 lb 3 oz **large frozen peeled shrimp**, defrosted

1 teaspoon **sesame oil**

2 tablespoons **light soy sauce**

1 tablespoon **honey**

1 teaspoon grated **fresh ginger root**

1 teaspoon crushed **garlic**

1 tablespoon **lemon juice**

1 lb **bok choy**

2 tablespoons **vegetable oil**

salt and pepper

Put the shrimp in a glass or ceramic bowl. Add the sesame oil, soy sauce, honey, ginger, garlic, and lemon juice. Season to taste with salt and pepper and mix well, then cover and allow to marinate in a cool place for 5–10 minutes.

Cut the heads of bok choy in half lengthwise, then blanch in a large saucepan of boiling water for 40–50 seconds. Drain well, cover, and keep warm.

Heat the vegetable oil in a wok or large skillet. Add the shrimp and marinade and stir-fry over a high heat for 2 minutes until thoroughly hot.

Divide the bok choy between 4 serving plates, then top with the shrimp and any juices from the pan. Serve immediately.

For sesame chicken with broccoli & red pepper,

use 1 lb 3 oz boneless, skinless chicken breast, cut into thin strips, in place of the shrimp. Coat with the marinade as above, then cover and allow to marinate in the refrigerator for 1–2 hours. Meanwhile, trim the stalks from 13 oz broccoli. Divide the heads into small florets, then peel and diagonally slice the stalks. Blanch the florets and stalks in a large saucepan of salted boiling water for 30 seconds. Drain well, refresh under cold running water, and drain again thoroughly. Core, seed, and thinly slice 1 large red bell pepper. Heat the oil in the wok or large skillet as above, add the chicken and marinade, and stir-fry over a high heat for 2 minutes. Add the broccoli and red pepper and stir-fry for an additional 2 minutes. Serve immediately.

egg pots with smoked salmon

Serves **4**
Preparation time **5 minutes**
Cooking time **10–15 minutes**

7 oz **smoked salmon trimmings**
2 tablespoons chopped **chives**
4 **eggs**
4 tablespoons **heavy cream**
toasted bread, to serve
pepper

Divide the smoked salmon and chives between 4 buttered ramekins. Make a small indent in the salmon with the back of a spoon and break an egg into the hollow, sprinkle with a little pepper, and spoon the cream over the top.

Put the ramekins in a roasting pan and half-fill the pan with boiling water. Bake in a preheated oven, 350°F, for 10–15 minutes or until the eggs have just set.

Remove from the oven and allow to cool for a few minutes, then serve with the toasted bread.

For homemade Melba toast, to serve with the baked egg pots, toast 4 slices of bread lightly on both sides. While hot, trim off the crusts, then split the toast in half widthwise. Lay the toast, cut-side up, on a baking sheet and bake in the bottom of the oven with the egg pots until dry.

fish kebabs & scallion mash

Serves **4**
Preparation time **15 minutes**,
 plus marinating
Cooking time **18–20 minutes**

1 lb 3 oz **skinless haddock
 or cod**, cut into 1 inch cubes
½ cup **plain yogurt**
1 teaspoon crushed **garlic**
1 teaspoon grated **fresh
 ginger root**
1 teaspoon **hot chili powder**
1 tablespoon **ground
 coriander**
1 tablespoon **ground cumin**

For the scallion mash
6 large **round white
 potatoes**, diced
⅔ cup **sour cream**
4 tablespoons finely chopped
 cilantro leaves
1 **red chili**, seeded and thinly
 sliced
4 **scallions**, thinly sliced
salt and pepper

Lay the fish cubes in a large, shallow glass or ceramic
dish. In a small bowl, mix together the yogurt, garlic,
ginger, chili powder, ground coriander, and cumin.
Season the mixture to taste and pour over the fish.
Cover and allow to marinate in a cool place while you
make the mash.

Cook the potatoes in a large saucepan of salted boiling
water for 10 minutes or until tender. Drain in a colander
and return to the pan. Mash the potatoes and add the
sour cream. Continue mashing until smooth, then stir in
the chopped cilantro, chili, and scallions. Season to taste
with salt and pepper, cover, and set aside.

Heat the broiler on the hottest setting. Thread the
cubes of fish evenly onto 4 metal skewers and cook
under the broiler for 8–10 minutes, turning once. Serve
immediately, with the mash and a green salad.

For spinach mash, to serve as an alternative
accompaniment, while the potatoes are cooking, heat
2 tablespoons oil in a saucepan, add 1 finely chopped
onion and 1 finely chopped garlic clove, and cook for
5 minutes. Add 4 cups chopped spinach leaves and
cook, stirring, for 2 minutes or until the spinach just
starts to wilt. Stir in 1 teaspoon ground ginger. Mash the
potatoes with the spinach mixture and 4 tablespoons
milk. Season to taste with salt and pepper.

mackerel with avocado salsa

Serves **4**
Preparation time **10 minutes**
Cooking time **6–8 minutes**

8 **mackerel fillets**
2 **lemons**, plus extra wedges
  to serve
salt and pepper

For the avocado salsa
2 **avocados**, peeled, pitted,
  and finely diced
juice and zest of **1 lime**
1 **red onion**, finely chopped
½ **cucumber**, finely diced
1 handful of **cilantro leaves**,
  finely chopped

Make 3 diagonal slashes across each mackerel fillet on the skin side and season well with salt and pepper. Cut the lemons in half, then squeeze the juice over the fish.

Lay on a broiler rack, skin-side up, and cook under a preheated broiler for 6–8 minutes or until the skin is lightly charred and the flesh is just cooked through.

Meanwhile, to make the salsa, mix together the avocados and lime juice and zest, then add the onion, cucumber, and cilantro. Toss well to mix and season to taste with salt and pepper.

Serve the mackerel hot with the avocado salsa and lemon wedges for squeezing over.

For broiled sardines with tomato relish, replace the mackerel fillets with 12 whole, cleaned and gutted sardines and broil for 4–5 minutes on each side. Meanwhile, put the chopped white parts of 4 scallions, 2 tablespoons lime juice, 8 oz ripe tomatoes, skinned, seeded, and chopped, ½ chopped sundried tomato, 1 seeded and chopped red chili, and 3 tablespoons chopped cilantro leaves in a food processor or blender and process until well combined. Serve the sardines hot with the relish.

salmon with lime zucchini

Serves **4**
Preparation time **10 minutes**
Cooking time **10–15 minutes**

4 **salmon fillet** portions, about
  7 oz each
1 tablespoon prepared
  English mustard
1 teaspoon grated **fresh
  ginger root**
1 teaspoon crushed **garlic**
2 teaspoons **honey**
1 tablespoon **light soy sauce**
  or **tamari**
salt and pepper

For the lime zucchini
2 tablespoons **olive oil**
1 lb **zucchini**, thinly sliced
  lengthwise
grated zest and juice of **1 lime**
2 tablespoons chopped **mint**

Lay the salmon fillet portions, skin-side down, in a shallow flameproof dish, to fit snugly in a single layer. In a small bowl, mix together the mustard, ginger, garlic, honey, and soy sauce or tamari, then spoon evenly over the fillets. Season to taste with salt and pepper.

Heat the broiler on the hottest setting. Cook the salmon fillets under the broiler for 10–15 minutes, until lightly charred on top and cooked through.

Meanwhile, to prepare the lime zucchini, heat the oil in a large nonstick skillet, add the zucchini, and cook, stirring frequently, for 5–6 minutes or until lightly browned and tender. Stir in the lime zest and juice and mint and season to taste with salt and pepper.

Serve the salmon hot with the zucchini.

For stir-fried green beans to serve in place of the lime zucchini, cut 1 lb green beans into 2 inch lengths. Heat 2 tablespoons vegetable oil in a wok or large skillet, add 2 crushed garlic cloves, 1 teaspoon grated fresh ginger root, and 2 thinly sliced shallots and stir-fry over a medium heat for 1 minute. Add the beans and ½ teaspoon salt and stir-fry over a high heat for 1 minute. Add 1 tablespoon light soy sauce and ⅔ cup chicken or vegetable stock and bring to a boil. Reduce the heat and cook, stirring frequently, for an additional 4 minutes, or until the beans are tender and the liquid has thickened. Season with pepper and serve immediately with the salmon.

spiced calamari with parsley salad

Serves **4**

Preparation time **15 minutes**, plus standing

Cooking time **about 5 minutes**

1 cup **besan** (chickpea or gram flour)

1½ teaspoons **paprika**

1½ teaspoons **ground cumin**

½ teaspoon **baking powder**

¼ teaspoon **pepper**

1 cup **soda water**

vegetable oil, for deep-frying

6 **whole squid**, cleaned and cut into ½ inch thick rings

salt

For the parsley salad

4 tablespoons **lemon juice**

4 tablespoons **olive oil**

2 **garlic cloves**, finely chopped

3 tablespoons **flat-leaf parsley**

1 **red onion**, halved and thinly sliced

2 **tomatoes**, roughly chopped

Sift the besan, paprika, cumin, and baking powder into a bowl, add the pepper, and mix together. Make a well in the center. Gradually add the soda water and beat until it is a smooth batter. Season to taste with salt. Cover and allow to stand for 30 minutes.

Meanwhile, for the salad dressing, in a bowl, beat together the lemon juice, olive oil, and garlic.

Fill a deep, heavy saucepan one-third full with vegetable oil and heat until a cube of bread browns in 15 seconds. Dip the squid rings in the batter, add to the oil, in batches, and cook for 30−60 seconds until golden brown. Remove with a slotted spoon and drain on paper towels.

Add the parsley, red onion, and tomatoes to the dressing and toss well to mix. Top with the battered squid and serve immediately.

For pan-fried squid with chili, slit the bodies of the squid down one side and lay flat, inside up. Using a sharp knife, score the flesh with a criss-cross pattern. Cut any tentacles into small pieces. In a bowl, mix together 2 tablespoons olive oil, 3 crushed garlic cloves, 1 finely chopped red chili, and 4 tablespoons lemon juice. Add the squid, cover, and allow to marinate in a cool place for 15 minutes. Remove the squid from the marinade. Heat 2 tablespoons olive oil in a large skillet until just smoking, add the squid, and season to taste with salt and pepper. Cook, stirring, over a high heat for 2−3 minutes until browned. Strain the marinade and stir into the pan with 2 tablespoons finely chopped flat-leaf parsley.

shrimp & crab cakes with chili jam

Serves **4**

Preparation time **15 minutes**, plus cooling and chilling

Cooking time **15 minutes**

2 x 6 oz cans **white crabmeat**

grated zest and juice of **1 lime**

4 **scallions**, chopped

1 **red chili**, seeded and finely chopped

1 teaspoon grated **fresh ginger root**

1 teaspoon crushed **garlic**

3 tablespoons chopped **cilantro leaves**, plus extra leaves to garnish

3 tablespoons **mayonnaise**

2 cups **fresh white bread crumbs**

7 oz **frozen cooked peeled shrimp**, defrosted

salt and pepper

vegetable oil, for pan-frying

For the chili jam

2 **red chilies**, seeded and finely diced

6 tablespoons **superfine sugar**

2 tablespoons **water**

Put the crabmeat, lime zest and juice, scallions, chili, ginger, garlic, cilantro, mayonnaise, and bread crumbs in a food processor and process until well combined. Transfer the mixture to a bowl. Chop the shrimp and fold into the mixture with salt and pepper to taste. Alternatively, the ingredients can be mixed together by hand. Cover and chill while making and cooling the chili jam.

Put all the chili jam ingredients in a small saucepan and heat gently until simmering. Cook for 4–5 minutes until the sugar has dissolved and the mixture has thickened slightly. Allow to cool.

Form the shrimp mixture into 12 cakes.

Heat the oil in a large nonstick skillet, add the cakes, and cook for 3–4 minutes on each side or until golden. Drain on paper towels and serve immediately garnished with cilantro leaves. Serve the chili jam spooned over the cakes or separately. A crisp arugula salad or green salad is a good accompaniment.

For coconut cilantro sauce to serve as an alternative to the chili jam, put 1 cup coconut milk, 2 tablespoons smooth peanut butter, 2 finely chopped scallions, white parts only, 1 crushed garlic clove, 1 finely chopped green chili, 2 tablespoons chopped cilantro leaves, 1 tablespoon lime juice, and 1 teaspoon sugar in a food processor or blender and process until smooth.

trout with cucumber relish

Serves **4**
Preparation time **10 minutes**
Cooking time **10–12 minutes**

4 **rainbow trout**, cleaned
  and gutted
1 tablespoon **sesame oil**
crushed **Szechuan pepper**,
  to taste
salt

For the cucumber relish
1 **cucumber**, about 8 inches
  long
2 teaspoons **salt**
4 tablespoons **rice vinegar**
3 tablespoons **superfine
  sugar**
1 **red chili**, seeded and sliced
1¼ inch piece **fresh ginger
  root**, peeled and grated
4 tablespoons **cold water**

To garnish
chopped chives
lemon wedges

Cut the cucumber in half lengthwise, scoop out and discard the seeds and cut the flesh into ½ inch slices. Put in a glass or ceramic bowl. In a small bowl, put the salt, vinegar, sugar, chili, and ginger, add the water and mix well. Pour over the cucumber, cover, and allow to marinate at room temperature while you cook the trout.

Brush the trout with the oil and season to taste with crushed Szechuan pepper and salt. Place the trout in a single layer on a broiler rack and broil for 5–6 minutes on each side or until cooked through. Allow to rest for a few moments, then garnish with chopped chives and serve with the cucumber relish and lemon wedges.

For trout with ground almond dressing, brush the trout with 1 tablespoon olive oil and season to taste with salt and black pepper. While the trout is cooking as above, put 1 cup ground almonds in a small saucepan over a medium heat and cook, stirring constantly, until lightly browned. Remove from the heat, add 6 tablespoons olive oil, 4 tablespoons lemon juice, and 2 tablespoons chopped parsley, and season to taste with salt and pepper. Stir well, then return to the heat for 2 minutes. Pour the dressing over the cooked trout, garnish with parsley sprigs, and serve immediately.

summer shrimp & fish phyllo pie

Serves **4**
Preparation time **10 minutes**
Cooking time **20–25 minutes**

1½ lb **skinless white fish fillets**
4 oz **frozen cooked peeled shrimp**, defrosted
⅔ cup **frozen peas**, defrosted
grated zest and juice of
  1 **lemon**
2½ cups **bottled white sauce**
1 bunch of **dill weed**, chopped
8 sheets of **phyllo pastry**
melted butter, for brushing
salt and pepper

Cut the fish into large, bite-size pieces and put in a bowl with the shrimp and peas. Add the lemon zest and juice, stir in the white sauce and dill weed, and season well with salt and pepper.

Tip the fish mixture into 4 individual gratin or pie dishes. Cover the surface of each pie with 2 sheets of phyllo pastry, scrunching up each sheet into a loosely crumpled ball. Brush the pastry with melted butter.

Bake in a preheated oven, 400°F, for 20–25 minutes until the pastry is golden brown and the fish is cooked through.

For seafood & potato pie, prepare the fish mixture as above, but use 2 tablespoons chopped parsley in place of the dill weed. Put into a medium ovenproof dish. Cook 1 lb 10 oz chopped potatoes in a large saucepan of salted boiling water until tender. Meanwhile, put 2 large eggs in a separate saucepan and bring to a boil. Cook for 10 minutes, then plunge into cold water to cool. Shell the eggs and cut in half lengthwise. Drain the potatoes and mash with 2 tablespoons butter. Season well with salt and pepper. Gently press the egg halves, at evenly spaced intervals, into the fish mixture, then spoon or pipe the mash over the fish mixture. Bake in a preheated oven, 400°F, for 20–25 minutes or until the top is lightly golden.

creamy shrimp curry

Serves **4**

Preparation time **10 minutes**

Cooking time **about
10 minutes**

2 tablespoons **vegetable oil**
1 **onion**, halved and finely
   sliced
2 **garlic cloves**, finely sliced
1 inch piece of **fresh ginger
   root**, peeled and finely
   chopped
1 tablespoon **ground
   coriander**
1 tablespoon **ground cumin**
½ teaspoon **turmeric**
¾ cup **coconut milk**
½ cup **vegetable stock**
1 lb 3 oz **frozen large cooked
   peeled shrimp**, defrosted
grated zest and juice of **1 lime**
4 tablespoons finely chopped
   cilantro leaves
salt and pepper

Heat the oil in a large saucepan, add the onion, garlic,
and ginger and cook for 4–5 minutes. Add the ground
coriander, cumin, and turmeric and cook, stirring, for
1 minute.

Pour in the coconut milk and stock and bring to a boil.
Reduce the heat and simmer for 2–3 minutes. Stir in
the shrimp and lime zest and juice, then simmer for
2 minutes or until the shrimp are heated through.

Stir in the chopped cilantro and season well with salt
and pepper. Serve immediately with boiled basmati or
jasmine rice.

For spiced coconut rice to serve with the curry, rinse
1½ cups basmati rice in cold water until the water
runs clear. Drain and put in a large, heavy saucepan.
Dissolve ½ cup chopped creamed coconut in 3 cups
boiling water and add to the rice with a 3 inch piece
of lemon grass stalk, halved lengthwise, 2 x 1 inch
pieces of cinnamon stick, 1 teaspoon salt, and pepper
to taste. Bring the rice to a boil, then cover and cook
for 10 minutes until almost all the liquid has been
absorbed. Turn off the heat and allow to stand for
10 minutes until the rice is tender. Fluff up with a
fork before serving with the curry.

red salmon & roasted vegetables

Serves **4**

Preparation time **10 minutes**

Cooking time **25 minutes**

1 **eggplant**, cut into bite-size
   pieces

2 **red bell peppers**, cored,
   seeded, and cut into
   bite-size pieces

2 **red onions**, quartered

1 **garlic clove**, crushed

4 tablespoons **olive oil**

pinch of **dried oregano**

7 oz can **red salmon**, drained
   and flaked

½ cup **pitted black olives**

salt and pepper

basil leaves, to garnish

Mix together the eggplant, red peppers, onions, and garlic in a bowl with the oil and oregano and season well with salt and pepper.

Spread the vegetables out in a single layer in a nonstick roasting pan and roast in a preheated oven, 425°F, for 25 minutes or until the vegetables are just cooked.

Transfer the vegetables to a warmed serving dish and gently toss in the salmon and olives. Serve warm or at room temperature, garnished with basil leaves.

For arugula & cucumber couscous to serve with the salmon and vegetables, put 1 cup instant couscous in a large, heatproof bowl. Season well with salt and pepper and pour over boiling hot water to just cover the couscous. Cover and allow to stand for 10–12 minutes until all the water has been absorbed. Meanwhile, finely chop 4 scallions, halve, seed, and chop ½ cucumber and chop 2 cups arugula leaves. Fluff up the couscous grains with a fork and tip into a warmed serving dish. Stir in the prepared ingredients with 2 tablespoons olive oil and 1 tablespoon lemon juice. Toss well to mix and serve with the salmon and vegetables.

tuna niçoise spaghetti

Serves **4**
Preparation time **10 minutes**
Cooking time **10 minutes**

4 **eggs**
12 oz **dried spaghetti**
3 x 7 oz cans **tuna in brine**, drained
4 oz **green beans**, trimmed and blanched
½ cup **kalamata olives**, pitted
1½ cups **semidried tomatoes**
1 teaspoon grated **lemon zest**
2 tablespoons **lemon juice**
3 tablespoons **capers**
salt and pepper

Put the eggs in a saucepan of cold water and bring to a boil. Cook for 10 minutes, then plunge into cold water to cool. Shell the eggs, then roughly chop and set aside.

Meanwhile, cook the pasta in a large saucepan of salted boiling water according to the package instructions until al dente.

Mix together the tuna, beans, olives, semidried tomatoes, lemon zest and juice, and capers in a bowl. Season to taste with pepper.

Drain the pasta and return to the pan. Add the tuna mixture and gently toss to combine. Serve immediately garnished with the eggs.

For tuna, pea, & corn rice cook 1 cup easy-cook basmati rice in a large saucepan of lightly salted boiling water for 12–15 minutes or until tender. Drain, refresh under cold running water, and drain again. Meanwhile, cook the eggs as above, then shell and cut into quarters. In a separate saucepan, cook ⅔ cup frozen corn and ⅔ cup frozen peas in salted boiling water for 5 minutes or until tender. Drain, refresh under cold running water, and drain again. In a large bowl, mix together the rice, corn, and peas, together with the tuna and olives, as above, and 2 tablespoons chopped basil. Beat together 2 tablespoons lemon juice, 1 tablespoon olive oil, and 1 crushed garlic clove, add to the rice, and toss well to coat. Serve garnished with the egg quarters.

moroccan broiled sardines

Serves **4**
Preparation time **10 minutes**
Cooking time **6–8 minutes**

12 **sardines**, cleaned
  and gutted
2 tablespoons **harissa**
2 tablespoons **olive oil**
juice of **1 lemon**
salt flakes and pepper
chopped cilantro, to garnish
lemon wedges, to serve

Heat the broiler on the hottest setting. Rinse the sardines and pat dry with paper towels. Make 3 deep slashes on both sides of each fish with a sharp knife.

Mix the harissa with the oil and lemon juice to make a thin paste. Rub into the sardines on both sides. Put the sardines on a lightly oiled baking sheet. Cook under the broiler for 3–4 minutes on each side, depending on their size, or until cooked through. Season to taste with salt flakes and pepper and serve immediately garnished with cilantro and with lemon wedges for squeezing over.

For baked sardines with pesto, line a medium ovenproof dish with 2 sliced tomatoes and 2 sliced onions. Prepare the sardines as above, then rub 4 tablespoons pesto over the fish and arrange in a single layer on top of the tomatoes and onions. Cover with foil and bake in a preheated oven, 400°F, for 20–25 minutes or until the fish is cooked through.

thai-style coconut mussels

Serves **4**
Preparation time **20 minutes**
Cooking time **about
 10 minutes**

4 lb **fresh, live mussels**
2½ cups **vegetable stock**
1¾ cups **coconut milk**
grated zest and juice of
 2 limes
2 **lemon grass stalks**, lightly
 bruised, plus extra stalks
 to garnish (optional)
1 tablespoon **Thai green
 curry paste**
3 **red chilies**, seeded and
 finely sliced
4 tablespoons chopped
 cilantro leaves, plus extra
 to garnish (optional)
2 **scallions**, shredded
salt and pepper
1 **red chili,** seeded and
 chopped, to garnish
 (optional)

Scrub the mussels in cold water, scrape off any barnacles, and pull away the hairy beards that protrude from the shells. Discard any with broken shells or any open mussels that do not close when tapped sharply.

Pour the stock and coconut milk into a large saucepan and bring to a boil. Stir in the lime zest and juice, lemon grass, curry paste, chilies, cilantro, and scallions. Season to taste with salt and pepper.

Add the mussels, cover, and return to a boil. Cook for 3–4 minutes or until all the mussels have opened. Discard any shells that remain closed. Use a slotted spoon to divide the mussels between 4 serving bowls and keep warm until ready to serve.

Bring the liquid to a vigorous boil and boil rapidly for 5 minutes or until reduced. Strain through a fine sieve, then ladle over the mussels. Garnish with chopped red chili, chopped cilantro leaves, and lemon grass stalks.

For homemade Thai green curry paste, put 15 small green chilies, 4 halved garlic cloves, 2 finely chopped lemon grass stalks, 2 torn lime leaves, 2 chopped shallots, 2 oz cilantro leaves, stalks, and roots, 1 inch piece of fresh ginger root, peeled and finely chopped, 2 teaspoons black peppercorns, 1 teaspoon pared lime peel, ½ teaspoon salt, and 1 tablespoon peanut oil into a food processor or blender and process to a thick paste. Alternatively, use a mortar and pestle to crush the ingredients, working in the oil at the end. Transfer the paste to an airtight container; it can be stored in a refrigerator for up to 3 weeks.

desserts

pineapple with lime & chili syrup

Serves **4**

Preparation time **10 minutes**, plus cooling

Cooking time **10 minutes**

½ cup **superfine sugar**

½ cup **water**

3 **red chilies**

grated zest and juice of 1 **lime**

1 **baby pineapple**, halved or quartered, cored, and cut into wafer-thin slices

Put the sugar in a saucepan with the water. Heat slowly until the sugar has dissolved, then add the chilies, bring to a boil, and boil rapidly until the liquid becomes syrupy. Allow to cool.

Stir the lime zest and juice into the cooled syrup. Lay the pineapple slices on a plate and drizzle the syrup over. Serve chilled with a dollop of ice cream, if desired.

For pears with cinnamon syrup, peel 4 ripe pears, cut into quarters, and remove the cores. Put in a saucepan, pour over water to cover, and add the superfine sugar as above, together with the grated zest and juice of 1 lemon, 1 cinnamon stick, and 6 cloves. Simmer, turning occasionally, for 10 minutes or until tender. Remove the pears with a slotted spoon and set aside. Bring the liquid to a boil and boil rapidly until the liquid becomes syrupy. Allow to cool, then pour over the pears.

tipsy berry waffles

Serves **4**
Preparation time **5 minutes**
Cooking time **1–2 minutes**

1 tablespoon **butter**
2 cups **mixed berries**, such
  as blueberries, blackberries,
  and raspberries
1 tablespoon **superfine sugar**
2 tablespoons **kirsch**
4 **waffles**
4 tablespoons **sour cream**

Melt the butter in a nonstick skillet, add the berries, sugar, and kirsch and cook over a high heat, stirring gently, for 1–2 minutes.

Meanwhile, toast or reheat the waffles according to the package instructions. Put a waffle on each serving plate, spoon the berries over the waffles, and top each portion with 1 tablespoon sour cream. Serve immediately.

For homemade waffles, sift 1 cup all-purpose flour, 1 teaspoon baking powder, and a pinch of salt into a bowl. Make a well in the center and gradually beat in 2 eggs and ⅔ cup milk until the batter is thick and smooth. Just before cooking, beat in 3 tablespoons cooled melted butter. Heat a waffle iron and oil if necessary. Spoon in enough batter to give a good coating, close, and cook for about 1 minute on each side. Lift the lid and remove the waffle. Repeat with the remaining batter.

apricot tartlets

Serves **4**
Preparation time **15 minutes**
Cooking time **20–25 minutes**

12 oz **ready-rolled puff
  pastry**, defrosted if frozen
½ cup **marzipan**
12 canned **apricot halves**,
  drained
light brown sugar, for
  sprinkling
apricot jelly, for glazing

Using a saucer as a template, cut 4 rounds from the pastry, each approximately 3½ inches in diameter. Score a line about ½ inch from the edge of each round with a sharp knife.

Roll out the marzipan to ⅛ inch thick and cut out 4 rounds to fit inside the scored circles. Lay the pastry rounds on a baking sheet, place a circle of marzipan in the center of each, and arrange 3 apricot halves, cut-side up, on top. Sprinkle a little sugar into each apricot.

Put the baking sheet on top of a second preheated baking sheet (this helps to crisp the pastry bases) and bake in a preheated oven, 400°F, for 20–25 minutes until the pastry is puffed and browned and the apricots are slightly caramelized around the edges. While still hot, brush the tops with apricot jelly to glaze. Serve immediately.

For banana tartlets with rum mascarpone, follow the recipe above, but use 2 thickly sliced bananas in place of the apricots. While the tartlets are baking, in a bowl, mix together 4 tablespoons mascarpone cheese, 2 tablespoons rum, and 2 tablespoons light brown sugar. Spoon on top of the hot tartlets and serve immediately.

hot berry soufflés

Serves **4**
Preparation time **10 minutes**
Cooking time **15 minutes**

1 tablespoon **butter**
½ cup **superfine sugar**
⅛ cup **blackberries**
1⅔ cups **raspberries**
4 **large egg whites**
confectioners' sugar, for
    dusting (optional)

Use the butter to grease 4 x ¾ cup ramekins and then coat evenly with a little of the superfine sugar, tipping out the excess sugar. Set the ramekins on a baking sheet.

Puree the blackberries and raspberries in a food processor or blender, reserving a few of the berries to decorate, then pour the puree into a bowl. Alternatively, the berries can be rubbed through a fine sieve to make a smooth puree.

Beat the egg whites until stiff but not dry in a large, perfectly clean bowl. Gradually sprinkle in the remaining superfine sugar, whisking continuously, and continue whisking until the whites are stiff and shiny.

Gently fold the egg whites into the berry puree, then spoon the mixture into the prepared ramekins. Bake immediately in a preheated oven, 375°F, for 15 minutes or until risen and golden.

Dust the soufflés with confectioners' sugar and decorate with the reserved berries. Serve immediately, with custard or ice cream, if desired.

For homemade custard to serve as an accompaniment, gently heat 1¼ cups milk in a saucepan without boiling. Meanwhile, beat 2 egg yolks in a bowl with 1 tablespoon sugar and a few drops of vanilla extract, then pour the milk into the bowl, stirring constantly. Return the mixture to the pan and heat over a low heat, stirring constantly, until the custard thickens enough to coat the back of the spoon. Serve immediately with the soufflés.

strawberry cheesecake pots

Serves **4**
Preparation time **15 minutes**,
   plus cooling and chilling
Cooking time **5 minutes**

2 tablespoons **butter**
5 **graham crackers**
1 cup **strawberries**
2 tablespoons **superfine
   sugar**
1 cup **mascarpone cheese**
4 tablespoons **heavy cream**
4 tablespoons **confectioners'
   sugar**
grated zest and juice of
   1 **lemon**

Melt the butter in a small saucepan, then transfer to a food processor with the graham crackers and process to fine crumbs. Divide the mixture between 4 glasses and press into the base of each. Chill in the refrigerator.

Meanwhile, put the strawberries and superfine sugar in a saucepan and cook, stirring, for 2–3 minutes, then allow to cool. In a bowl, mix together the mascarpone, cream, confectioners' sugar, and lemon zest and juice.

Fill the glasses with the mascarpone mixture and top each with the strawberries. Chill for 2–3 hours before serving.

For ginger raspberry cheesecake pots, follow the recipe above, but use gingersnap cookies in place of the graham crackers, raspberries instead of strawberries, and thick yogurt in place of the mascarpone. Sprinkle the top of each dessert with 1 teaspoon chopped stem ginger.

walnut & white chocolate cookies

Makes **about 25**
Preparation time **15 minutes,**
  plus cooling
Cooking time **12–15 minutes**

1 **egg**
⅔ cup **light brown sugar**
2 tablespoons **superfine**
  sugar
1 teaspoon **vanilla extract**
½ cup **vegetable oil**
½ cup **all-purpose flour**
3 tablespoons **self-rising**
  flour
¼ teaspoon **ground cinnamon**
⅓ cup **shredded coconut**
1½ cups **walnuts**, toasted
  and chopped
⅔ cup **white chocolate chips**

Grease 2 baking sheets and line with nonstick parchment paper. In a bowl, beat the egg and sugars together until light and creamy. Stir in the vanilla extract and oil. Sift in the flours and cinnamon, then add the coconut, walnuts, and chocolate and mix well with a wooden spoon.

Form rounded tablespoonfuls of the mixture into balls and place on the prepared baking sheets, pressing the mixture together with your fingertips if it is crumbly. Bake in a preheated oven, 350°F, for 12–15 minutes or until golden. Allow to cool slightly on the sheets, then transfer to a cooling rack to cool completely.

For hazelnut & chocolate chip cookies, follow the recipe above but use ½ teaspoon ground ginger in place of the cinnamon, 1¼ cups toasted and chopped hazelnuts instead of the walnuts, and semisweet chocolate chips in place of the white.

fig & honey pots

Serves **4**

Preparation time **10 minutes**, plus chilling

6 **ripe fresh figs**, thinly sliced, plus 2 extra, cut into wedges, to decorate (optional)

1¾ cups **Greek** or **whole milk yogurt**

4 tablespoons **honey**

2 tablespoons chopped **pistachio nuts**

Arrange the fig slices snugly in the bottom of 4 glasses or glass bowls. Spoon the yogurt over the figs and chill in the refrigerator for 10–15 minutes.

Just before serving, drizzle 1 tablespoon honey over each dessert and sprinkle the pistachio nuts on top. Decorate with the wedges of fig, if desired.

For hot figs with honey, heat a griddle pan, add 8 whole ripe fresh figs and cook for 8 minutes, turning occasionally, until charred on the outside. Alternatively, cook under a preheated broiler. Remove and cut in half. Divide between 4 plates, top each with a tablespoonful of yogurt and drizzle with a little honey.

rhubarb slumps

Serves **4**
Preparation time **10 minutes**
Cooking time **20–25 minutes**

13 oz **rhubarb**, cut into
  chunks
6 tablespoons **superfine
  sugar**
grated zest and juice of
  1 orange
1 cup rolled **oats**
6 tablespoons **heavy cream**
2 tablespoons **dark brown
  sugar**

Mix together the rhubarb, superfine sugar, and orange zest and half the juice in a bowl. Spoon the mixture into 4 individual ramekins.

Put the oats, cream, dark brown sugar, and remaining orange juice in the bowl and mix together. Drop spoonfuls of the oat mixture all over the surface of the rhubarb mixture.

Set the ramekins on a baking sheet and bake in a preheated oven, 350°F, for 20–25 minutes until the topping is browned. Serve hot.

For apple and blackberry crumbles, peel, core, and chop 2 dessert apples, then mix with ⅔ cup blackberries, 6 tablespoons superfine sugar, and 1 tablespoon apple juice. Spoon into the ramekins as above. Sift 1 cup all-purpose flour into a bowl, add ¼ cup diced butter and blend with the fingertips until the mixture resembles coarse bread crumbs. Stir in ¼ cup dark brown sugar, ¾ cup bran flakes, and ⅓ cup chopped mixed nuts. Spoon the mixture over the fruit and flatten slightly with the back of a spoon. Bake as above until the topping is lightly golden.

chocolate chip cookies

Makes **16**
Preparation time **10 minutes,**
   plus cooling
Cooking time **15 minutes**

½ cup **unsalted butter**, diced
   and softened
¾ cup **light brown sugar**
1 teaspoon **vanilla extract**
1 **egg**, lightly beaten
1 tablespoon **milk**
1¾ cups **all-purpose flour**
1 teaspoon **baking powder**
1½ cups **semisweet**
   chocolate chips

Line a large baking sheet with nonstick parchment paper. In a large bowl, beat the butter and sugar together until light and fluffy. Mix in the vanilla extract, then gradually beat in the egg, beating well after each addition. Stir in the milk.

Sift the flour and baking powder into a separate large bowl, then fold into the butter and egg mixture. Stir in the chocolate chips.

Drop level tablespoonfuls of the cookie mixture on to the prepared baking sheet, leaving about 1½ inches between each cookie, then lightly press with a floured fork. Bake in a preheated oven, 350°F, for 15 minutes or until lightly golden. Transfer to a cooling rack to cool.

For chocolate & mandarin log, drain a 10 oz can mandarin segments and finely chop, reserving a few whole segments for decoration. In a bowl, whip 1¼ cups heavy cream with ¼ cup confectioners' sugar until thick, then fold in the chopped mandarins. Sandwich the cooked chocolate chip cookies one on top of the other with half the mandarin cream, then carefully set the log on its side and wrap in foil. Chill in the refrigerator for at least 2–3 hours or overnight. Just before serving, put the log on a serving plate, cover with the remaining mandarin cream, and decorate with the reserved mandarins. Serve in slices, cut on the diagonal.

caramelized banana puff tart

Serves **4**
Preparation time **10 minutes**
Cooking time **15–20 minutes**

3 **bananas**, sliced
12 oz **ready-made puff
pastry**, defrosted if frozen
1 **egg**, beaten
3 tablespoons **Demerara
sugar**
1¼ cups **whipping cream**
(optional)

Slice the bananas in half horizontally. Roll the pastry into an 8 inch square and cut the pastry into equal quarters. Place on a baking sheet and score a ½ inch border around the edge of each pastry square. Arrange the bananas, cut-side up, on the pastry inside the border, then brush the border with the beaten egg. Sprinkle the top of the bananas with the sugar.

Bake in a preheated oven, 400°F, for 15–20 minutes or until the pastry is puffed and golden and the bananas are caramelized. Serve the tart hot with cream.

For cinnamon coffee liqueur cream as an alternative accompaniment to the tart, in a bowl whip ¾ cup heavy cream until soft peaks form, then stir in 2 teaspoons ground cinnamon and 2 tablespoons Bailey's Irish Cream or any other creamy coffee liqueur.

date chocolate torte

Serves **4**
Preparation time **10 minutes,**
   plus cooling
Cooking time **30 minutes**

1 cup **slivered almonds**
4 oz **semisweet chocolate,**
   roughly chopped
⅔ cup **dried ready-to-eat**
   dates, pitted
3 **egg whites**
½ cup **superfine sugar**, plus
   2 tablespoons for the
   topping
½ cup **whipping cream**
cocoa powder, to sprinkle

Grease a 9 inch springform pan and line with nonstick parchment paper. Put the almonds and chocolate in a food processor and pulse until finely chopped. Finely chop the dates with a knife.

Beat the egg whites in a large, perfectly clean bowl until soft peaks form. Slowly add the ½ cup sugar and continue beating until it has dissolved. Fold in the almond and chocolate mixture, then the dates. Spoon the mixture into the prepared pan and level the surface.

Bake in a preheated oven, 350°F, for 30 minutes or until set and starting to come away from the side. Allow to cool in the pan before carefully turning out onto a serving plate.

Whip the cream and the remaining 2 tablespoons sugar in a small bowl until soft peaks form. Using a spatula, spread the cream evenly over the top of the torte. Serve cut into thin slices and dusted with cocoa.

For iced date chocolate muffins, spoon the chocolate mixture into 12 large, deep muffin pans lined with paper bake cups and bake in a preheated oven, 350°F, for 20–25 minutes or until set. Transfer to a cooling rack to cool. Melt 3 oz chopped plain dark chocolate with 3 tablespoons butter in a heatproof bowl set over a saucepan of gently simmering water. Meanwhile, toast 4 tablespoons slivered almonds in a dry skillet, stirring constantly, until golden brown. Stir the chocolate mixture, then spoon over the muffins and sprinkle with the toasted almonds. Leave until set.

madeleines

Makes **14**
Preparation time **15 minutes,**
  plus cooling
Cooking time **12 minutes**

3 **eggs**
½ cup **superfine sugar**
1¼ cups **all-purpose flour**
½ cup **unsalted butter**, melted
grated zest of 1 **lemon**
grated zest of 1 **orange**

Brush a pan of madeleine molds with melted butter and coat with all-purpose flour, then tap the pan to remove the excess flour.

Beat the eggs and sugar in a bowl until thick and pale and the beater leaves a trail when lifted. Sift the flour, then gently fold into the egg mixture. Fold in the melted butter and lemon and orange zest. Spoon into the molds, leaving a little room for rising.

Bake in a preheated oven, 400°F, for 12 minutes or until golden and springy to the touch. Remove the madeleines from the pan and allow to cool on a cooling rack.

For quick sherry trifle, line the base of a dessert or trifle bowl with the madeleines and sprinkle with 2–3 tablespoons sweet sherry. Top with 2 cups defrosted frozen mixed berries and top that with ¾ cup custard. Whip ¾ cup heavy cream until soft peaks form and pipe or spoon over the top. Cover and chill in the refrigerator for 2–3 hours before serving.

coconut syllabub & almond brittle

Serves **4**

Preparation time **15 minutes**, plus cooling and chilling

Cooking time **about 10 minutes**

½ cup **granulated sugar**

½ cup **slivered almonds**, toasted

For the syllabub

¾ cup **coconut cream**

1¼ cups **heavy cream**

15 **cardamom seeds**, lightly crushed

2 tablespoons **superfine sugar**

To make the brittle, put the granulated sugar and almonds in a saucepan over a low heat. While the sugar melts, lightly oil a baking sheet. When the sugar has melted and turned golden, pour the mixture onto the baking sheet and allow to cool.

To make the syllabub, pour the coconut cream and heavy cream into a large bowl. Add the crushed cardamom seeds and superfine sugar, then lightly whip until just holding soft peaks.

Spoon the syllabub into 4 glasses and chill in the refrigerator. Meanwhile, lightly crack the brittle into irregular shards. When ready to serve, top the syllabub with some of the brittle and serve the remainder separately on the side.

For lemon syllabub, put the grated zest and juice of 1 lemon in a bowl with ½ cup white wine and 3 tablespoons superfine sugar. Cover and allow to soak for about 1 hour. Whip 1¼ cups heavy cream until it forms soft peaks, then gradually add the wine mixture and continue whipping until it holds its shape. In a separate, perfectly clean bowl, beat 1 egg white until stiff, then beat in 3 tablespoons superfine sugar. Carefully fold into the cream mixture and spoon into 4 glasses. Chill in the refrigerator before serving.

lemon cookies

Makes **18–20**
Preparation time **15 minutes,**
    plus cooling
Cooking time **15–20 minutes**

½ cup **unsalted butter,**
    diced and softened
½ cup **superfine sugar**
2 **egg yolks**
2 teaspoons grated **lemon
    zest**
1¼ cups **all-purpose flour**
⅔ cup **coarse cornmeal**
saffron, to sprinkle (optional)
confectioners' sugar,
    for dusting

Line a baking sheet with nonstick parchment paper. In a bowl, beat the butter and sugar together until light and fluffy. Mix in the egg yolks, lemon zest, flour, and cornmeal until a soft dough forms.

Roll out the dough on a lightly floured surface to ½ inch thick. Using a 2½ inch round cutter, cut out rounds from the dough, rerolling the trimmings. Transfer to the prepared baking sheet, then sprinkle with saffron, if desired, and bake in a preheated oven, 325°F, for 15–20 minutes or until lightly golden. Transfer to a cooling rack to cool, then dust with confectioners' sugar.

For no-cook lemon cheesecakes, roughly crush 10 of the above cookies and place them in the base of 4 dessert bowls or glasses. Beat together 1¼ cups cream cheese with the finely grated zest and juice of 1 lemon, ⅓ cup superfine sugar and ⅔ cup heavy cream. Spoon this mixture into the prepared glasses and chill for 1–2 hours before serving.

lemon & orange mousse

Serves **4**

Preparation time **15 minutes**, plus chilling

1¼ cups **heavy cream**

grated zest and juice of 1 **lemon**, plus extra finely pared strips of peel to decorate

grated zest and juice of ½ **orange**, plus extra finely pared strips of peel to decorate

¼ cup **superfine sugar**

2 **egg whites**

Whip together the cream, grated lemon and orange zest, and sugar in a large bowl until the mixture starts to thicken. Add the lemon and orange juices and beat again until the mixture thickens.

Whip, in a separate large, perfectly clean bowl, the egg whites until soft peaks form, then fold into the citrus mixture. Spoon the mousse into 4 glasses and chill in the refrigerator. Decorate with lemon and orange peel strips.

For raspberry mousse, puree 1⅔ cups raspberries in a food processor or blender, then pass through a fine sieve. In a large bowl, whip together the cream and sugar as above until the mixture starts to thicken, then add the sieved raspberry puree and whip again until thickened. Continue with the recipe as above, but decorate with whole raspberries and semisweet chocolate shavings, shaved from a bar using a swivel-bladed vegetable peeler.

mango & passion fruit fool

Serves **4**

Preparation time **15 minutes**, plus chilling

2 ripe **mangoes**, peeled and pitted
1 tablespoon chopped **mint**
juice of ½ **lime**
1 cup **heavy cream**
1 cup **Greek** or **whole milk yogurt**
2 **passion fruit**

Dice 1 mango and combine with the mint. Divide almost half the mango mixture between 4 small bowls, reserving a little for the topping.

Puree the remaining mango with the lime juice in a food processor or blender.

Beat the cream in a bowl until just holding soft peaks, then stir in the yogurt. Fold the cream mixture into the mango puree and swirl to marble.

Divide the cream mixture between the bowls and top with the reserved diced mango. Halve each passion fruit, then scoop the seeds of each half over each fool. Chill in the refrigerator until ready to serve.

For peach & amaretti fool, use a 13 oz can peach halves, drained and diced, in place of the mango, mix with 2 tablespoons toasted slivered almonds and divide between 4 small bowls. Follow the recipe as above until the final stage. Then omit the passion fruit and instead top each dessert with a roughly crushed amaretti cookie.

chocolate soufflés

Serves **4**
Preparation time **12 minutes**
Cooking time **about
15 minutes**

1 cup chopped **semisweet
chocolate**
⅔ cup **butter**, diced and
softened
6 **eggs**
¾ cup **superfine sugar**
1 cup **all-purpose flour**
confectioners' sugar, to dust

Butter 4 x ¾ cup ramekins. Melt the chocolate with the butter in a heatproof bowl set over a saucepan of gently simmering water.

Beat the eggs and sugar together in a bowl until very light and creamy. Sift the flour, then fold into the egg mixture. Fold in the chocolate mixture.

Divide the soufflé mixture between the prepared ramekins. Bake in a preheated oven, 350°F, for 8–12 minutes. The soufflés should rise and form a firm crust, but you want them still to be slightly runny in the center. Serve immediately dusted with confectioners' sugar, with ice cream or cream.

For homemade vanilla ice cream to serve with the soufflés, in a heatproof bowl, mix together 1 whole egg, 1 egg yolk, and 3 tablespoons superfine sugar. Bring 1 cup light cream gently to boiling point in a saucepan and pour onto the egg mixture, stirring vigorously. Strain, then stir in 1–2 drops vanilla extract. Allow to cool, then fold in ⅔ cup whipped heavy cream. Pour into a rigid freezerproof container. Cover, seal, and freeze for 1 hour. Remove and stir well, then refreeze until firm. Transfer to the refrigerator 20 minutes before serving to soften.

peach & raspberry tartlets

Serves **4**
Preparation time **15 minutes**
Cooking time **8–10 minutes**,
  plus cooling

1 tablespoon **butter**, melted
4 sheets of **phyllo pastry**,
  each about 10 inches square
½ cup **heavy cream**
1 tablespoon **light brown
  sugar**
2 **peaches**, peeled, halved,
  pitted, and diced
½ cup **raspberries**
confectioners' sugar,
  for dusting

Brush 4 deep muffin cups with the melted butter. Cut a sheet of phyllo pastry in half, then across into 4 equal-size squares. Use these phyllo squares to line 1 muffin cup, arranging at slightly different angles, pressing down well, and tucking the pastry into the cup neatly. Repeat with the remaining pastry to line the other muffin cups.

Bake the phyllo pastry tartlets in a preheated oven, 375°F, for 8–10 minutes or until golden. Carefully remove the tartlet cases from the cups and allow to cool on a cooling rack.

Whip the cream and brown sugar lightly in a bowl, until it holds its shape. Spoon into the tartlet cases and top with the peaches and raspberries. Dust with confectioners' sugar. Serve immediately.

For strawberry and blueberry tartlets, grease 4 deep muffin cups as above. From ready-rolled shortcrust pastry (defrosted if frozen), cut out 4 rounds large enough to line the muffin cups. Prick the bases all over with a fork. Bake in a preheated oven, 375°F, for 15 minutes or until golden brown. Carefully remove from the cups and allow to cool on a cooling rack. Lightly whip the cream with 1 tablespoon confectioners' sugar, then spoon into the tartlet cases. Top with ⅓ cup sliced strawberries and ½ cup blueberries. Dust with confectioners' sugar and serve immediately.

index

acknowledgments

Executive Editor: Nicola Hill
Editor: Ruth Wiseall
Executive Art Editor: Leigh Jones
Designer: Jo Tapper
Photographer: Stephen Conroy
Home Economist: Sunil Vijayaker
Props Stylist: Liz Hippisley
Production Manager: Carolin Stransky

Special photography: © Octopus Publishing Group Limited/Stephen Conroy
Other photography: © Octopus Publishing Group Limited/Frank Adam 57, 127; /Neil Mersh 18, 24, 30, 44, 61, 73, 77, 79, 85, 103, 109, 131, 139, 142, 171, 174, 179 182, 189, 196, 203, 207, 213, 225, 235; /William Reavell 97; /Gareth Sambridge 135.